THE ECONOMICS OF FISHING

The Economics of Big Business

This series of books provides short, accessible introductions to the economics of major business sectors. Each book focuses on one particular global industry and examines its business model, economic strategy, the determinants of profitability as well as the unique issues facing its economic future. More general cross-sector challenges, which may be ethical, technological or environmental, as well as wider questions raised by the concentration of economic power, are also explored. The series offers rigorous presentations of the fundamental economics underpinning key industries suitable for both course use and a professional readership.

Published

The Economics of Airlines
Volodymyr Bilotkach

The Economics of Arms
Keith Hartley

The Economics of Cars
Fabio Cassia and Matteo Ferrazzi

The Economics of Construction
Stephen Gruneberg and Noble Francis

The Economics of Fishing
Rögnvaldur Hannesson

The Economics of Music
Peter Tschmuck

The Economics of Oil and Gas
Xiaoyi Mu

THE ECONOMICS OF FISHING

RÖGNVALDUR HANNESSON

agenda
publishing

© Rögnvaldur Hannesson 2021

First edition published in 2021 by Agenda Publishing

Agenda Publishing Limited
The Core
Bath Lane
Newcastle Helix
Newcastle upon Tyne
NE4 5TF
www.agendapub.com

ISBN 978-1-78821-343-1 (hardcover)
ISBN 978-1-78821-344-8 (paperback)

British Library Cataloguing-in-Publication Data
A catalogue record for this book is available from the British Library

Typeset by Newgen Publishing UK
Printed and bound in the UK by CPI Group (UK) Ltd, Croydon, CR0 4YY

CONTENTS

1

INTRODUCTION

This book is directed primarily at business students who wish to learn about the economics of fisheries. It should be useful also for others who take an interest in the fishing industry, such as journalists, politicians and public administrators dealing with the fishing industry and fisheries management and all the issues that arise in that context. These issues can be complex. Fish often migrate over a wide area that extends over the jurisdiction of several sovereign states and into the high seas. The abundance of fish varies substantially over time, partly because of fishing, but even more so because of the variability of nature, for reasons often ill understood and unpredictable. This is a perfect set-up for frustrated expectations and conflicts between different industrial groups and sovereign states.

To understand these issues is a formidable task for scholars and scientists wielding the powerful tools of science: data gathering and formal analysis by mathematics and statistics. This book attempts to communicate the major lessons learned in a way that is accessible to people without much formal training in these disciplines. Formal analysis is mainly by graphs, but equations and manipulations of them cannot be entirely avoided if something meaningful is to be said, and occasionally some simple calculus is used. This should not be beyond the grasp of students of business administration or social sciences. The issues are illustrated with examples from fisheries in various parts of the world: fish stocks that have crashed; conflicts over jurisdiction at sea; and management innovations, such as individual fish quotas.

Sometimes one is left with the impression that the excitement over fisheries issues is way out of proportion to the economic importance of the industry. As an example, the newspapers of early 2020 carried articles to the effect that access to fishing in the waters of the United Kingdom might be an obstacle to a post-Brexit trade agreement with the European Union, despite the fact that the economic contribution of the fish involved is almost negligible for both parties. The fisheries of the United Kingdom are indeed unlikely to be sufficiently important to make or break trading relations with the European Union, but it may nevertheless be noted that the contribution of fisheries to gross domestic product (GDP) underrates the importance of fisheries as an industry. Incomes from fishing support manufacturing industries and services by way of demand for goods and services, but those activities are recorded under other headings.

World fisheries would not loom very large in world GDP even if we had numbers accessible that would measure that, but in some areas the fishing industry is a cornerstone industry; were it to disappear, much of the remaining economic activity would be at risk. In the small island states of Cape Verde, the Faeroe Islands, Greenland, Iceland, the Maldives, the Seychelles and Vanuatu, fish and fish products exceed 40 per cent of merchandise exports (FAO 2020: 73). The fishing industry is also an important source of food, and more so in some areas than others, depending on traditional access to fish and food habits. Unsurprisingly, the consumption of fish per capita in island states such as the Faeroe Islands, Iceland, Kiribati and the Maldives is much higher than in land-locked states such as Ethiopia, Mongolia and Tajikistan (FAO 2020: 68). In some parts of the world, some developing countries in particular, food from the sea is critical. With a world population that is still growing, the last thing we need is a decline of any of the food sources we currently have.

It is logical, therefore, to begin (Chapter 2) with an overview of world fisheries. How have they developed over time? As we shall see, world capture fisheries grew rather quickly from 1950 to the end of the 1980s, at an annualized rate of over 4 per cent; more rapidly than world population, which grew at about 2 per cent per year in the 1960s, but more slowly after that. After 1990 world capture fisheries stagnated, and the continued growth in world fish production since 1990 has come from aquaculture.

Behind this growth and subsequent stagnation lie stories of individual fish stocks. It has become fashionable in certain circles to talk about the crisis in world fisheries, but stagnation is hardly a crisis; it could instead be the consequence of having come to the end of the road as far as capturing fish is concerned and adjusting to that fact. Even so, some important fish stocks have crashed, some undoubtedly because of overfishing, but most have recovered, aided by a sharp curtailment of fish catches. Variability of the environment affecting the renewal of fish stocks is an important factor in these crashes, and such variability is a fact that the industry must live with. Stabilization of fish catches may be highly desirable, but impossible to achieve in many – and perhaps most – cases. In the next chapter, and Chapter 5, we shall see the stories of some of those crashes.

Fish products are widely traded, and such trade has increased over time. Some trade has arisen because fish processing is cheaper in low-income countries than in advanced industrialized ones. Modern freezing technology has made it possible to trade raw fish over wide distances for further processing without much loss of quality. Such trade, as well as trade in finished fish products, is facilitated by relatively low tariffs on fish products.

Consumers of the final products in rich countries typically purchase them in supermarkets flush with many different food items and would reject products that do not meet their requirements. Glitches in the supply chain ending with the final consumer can ruin the whole operation. This requires strong companies that can deal with any issue that may arise and have adequate control over the supply chain. This, in turn, has repercussions for how the whole industry is organized. Furthermore, consumers often are concerned about how the fish they buy has been produced: has it been captured, or farmed, with practices that neither harm the sustainability of the fish stocks nor cause environmental damage? Organizations issuing certificates to the effect that fish products have been produced in an environmentally acceptable way have arisen to meet this need, but their services are not free of charge, and, as counterparts, companies and fisheries management authorities with sufficient authority and economic muscle are needed. These issues are discussed at some length in Chapter 2. Even so, the seafood industry can hardly be characterized as dominated by large, vertically integrated firms with operations around the globe. There are many of those, and the development of markets is probably working in their favour, but the industry still consists of a multitude of firms large and small, many with decidedly local operations.

Fisheries versus aquaculture

Aquatic products, fish and others, have two distinctly different origins: capture of wild fish and farming of fish in pens, tanks or ponds in the sea or on land. Fish consumers do not necessarily make a distinction between captured and farmed fish, and the quantitative indicators published by the Food and Agriculture Organization of the United Nations (FAO) and others about the importance of fish as supply of food make no such distinction. This book is primarily about capture fisheries and the issues they raise, which are quite different from aquaculture; capture fisheries are a form of hunting, albeit usually technologically quite advanced, whereas fish farming is more similar to animal husbandry. As shown in Chapter 2, the growth in the supply of aquatic products has for about 30 years come from aquaculture: while capture fisheries have stagnated, the production of aquaculture grew at an annualized rate of almost 7 per cent from 1990 to 2018. It thus seems clear that a continued increase in the production of aquatic products will have to come from aquaculture rather than the capture fisheries.

It is appropriate, therefore, to discuss aquaculture at some length, even if this is not the primary purpose of this book. This is done in Chapter 3. The role of freshwater fish in aquaculture production is much greater than in capture fisheries, and so is also the production of aquatic plants, mainly seaweed. Marine fish, in a wide sense of the word, are the mainstay of capture fisheries, but a rather small part of farmed fish, even if we include salmon, which live both in freshwater and salt water and are classified as "diadromous" fish. The growth in the production of farmed fish in recent years is somewhat paradoxical, given the stagnation of the capture fisheries, as one might have thought that farmed fish depended on feed derived from capture fisheries. Not all farmed fish depend on such feed, however, and some farmed fish are not fed at all, but traditionally many types of farmed fish, such as salmon, were fed with products largely derived from captured fish. The growth in the production of farmed fish, salmon in particular, has long since outpaced the ability of the fishmeal and fish oil industry to deliver products that go into fish feed production, and in fact this industry has stagnated in terms of quantity produced. Instead, salmon feed is now largely produced with plant ingredients. The expansion of farmed fish is therefore not quite the same thing as getting more and more of our food supplies from the sea; feeding fish with plant-based products means that the product ultimately comes from the land, even if the animals happen to be kept in an aquatic environment. There is, needless to say, nothing wrong with this, as long as the transformation of feed into final edible products is competitive in economic terms and acceptable in terms of quality and food security. Neither is there anything wrong with using feed from captured fish to raise other fish in captivity, as long as it is economically competitive and acceptable in terms of quality, food security and environmental practice. These issues are discussed at some length in Chapter 3.

Much of Chapter 3 is devoted to salmon farming. Although it is only a small part of the entire aquaculture industry, it is an interesting case. It targets high-end markets, even if salmon prices are now low enough to make it a staple food item in rich countries. The evolution of the industry is an interesting story; it began because salmon was a luxury product, the price of which could cover the high costs of production, but the latter for a while came down about as rapidly as the price itself yielded to increasing volumes being put on the market. The salmon-farming industry has developed impressively, both technically and organizationally; the fish are now fed by automatic feeders dispensing pelleted feed, to a large extent made from plants and not fish. The growth of the fish has been enhanced through selective breeding. The market is dominated by large, vertically integrated firms with operations in several countries suitable for growing salmon and with sufficient financial muscles to handle diseases and environmental issues that might arise. Some diseases have been conquered with vaccines. An adverse regulatory environment has thwarted the development of this industry in the United States, whereas inappropriate regulations were relaxed in Norway at an early stage, making it possible for Norwegian firms to become leaders in an industry with operations in many countries. In Chile, the regulatory environment has from the beginning been benign, and Chile has for many years been the second largest producer of farmed salmon.

Capture fisheries

In Chapter 4, a simple model of capture fisheries is presented. It is a "biomass" model; the growth of a fish population depends on the total weight of fish in the population. This is a gross simplification, but sufficient to demonstrate some fundamental principles of fisheries economics. Without any control of access to fish stocks, they will be overexploited. Economic overexploitation means that too much of productive resources are used for catching the fish; too much manpower, too many boats, and too much of everything that goes with it: fishing gear, fuel and other things. The last boat is not paying for itself even if it fishes just as much as all the other boats; it takes some fish that other boats could have caught, and to find its net contribution this amount must be subtracted. Economic overexploitation is not necessarily the same as biological overexploitation, which is usually defined as driving fish stocks below the level that supports maximum sustainable yield. Ignoring environmental fluctuations, any given sustainable yield from a stock can be supported by two different stock levels, one above and one below the level producing maximum sustainable yield. Strange as it may seem, biological overexploitation can be justified, up to a point, if the cost per unit of fish is insensitive to the size of the exploited stock. The analysis of the simple biomass model is mainly graphical, supplemented by some basic mathematics. Even if this model is exceedingly simple and founded on restrictive assumptions, it is still sufficient for showing that open access will lead to overfishing, as well as to demonstrate the difference between overfishing and efficient exploitation and explain why it occurs.

Even if the simple biomass model is a useful pedagogical tool to convey some of the central lessons of fishery economics, it is less than adequate for analyses of the fish stocks of the real world, especially those for which detailed data are now routinely collected. The last part of Chapter 4 presents the age-structured model nowadays widely applied in fisheries science. This model is presented for the case in which stock growth is deterministic and no environmental fluctuations occur. Having understood the basic structure of the model, the application to an environment where a stock fluctuates over time for natural reasons, as well as being exposed to a variable rate of exploitation, is straightforward. The chapter ends with a presentation of the Ricker model, in which a new cohort of fish depends on the size of the parent cohort, originally developed for Pacific salmon.

Natural fluctuations

The fisheries models of Chapter 4 are deterministic: the growth and development over time of fish stocks are fully determined by the rate of exploitation they are subjected to. This means that they can be perfectly controlled by the rate of exploitation. A pristine stock will necessarily be run down by fishing, but, if the latter is within the limits of sustainability, the stock will be stabilized at a certain level. That level may be too low, for economic and other reasons, but the fish stock can always be rebuilt to whatever level desired by a suitable reduction in fishing.

This is not how the fish stocks of the real world behave. They live in a variable natural environment, which means that their growth and development over time can be widely different for any given rate of exploitation. The variability is mainly manifested in the size of new cohorts (recruitment) entering the stock. Examples of variable recruitment are shown in Chapter 4, but Chapter 5 discusses a number of examples of fish stock variability and crashes. Most have recovered, but sometimes it has taken decades, and the Northern cod of Newfoundland has not fully recovered after the crash in the early 1990s. Some stock crashes have taken the industry down with them, never to be built up again despite stock recovery (the California sardine). Other fisheries have bounced back after decades (Norwegian spring-spawning herring).

The 200-mile zone: a sea change

Nothing less than a revolution in the international law of the sea occurred in the 1970s. Unlike so many revolutions, this one was relatively peaceful and took place at a conference on the subject, organized by the United Nations (UN), that lasted ten years. But it had a longer history. For a long time the maritime powers of Europe – the United Kingdom in particular – promoted freedom of the seas, including freedom to fish up to three nautical miles from shore. Over the last century efforts were made to change this arrangement and establish national fishing zones where only boats from the coastal state or those that it authorized could fish. A limit of 12 miles from baselines closing off fiords and bays was for many years the main target of coastal states wanting to extend their jurisdiction at sea. How this developed into 200 miles is the topic of Chapter 6.

There is no doubt that the 200-mile limit has fundamentally changed the framework of fisheries management. Some fish stocks are wholly confined within the 200-mile zone of a single country. Others migrate between the zones of two or more countries and have, essentially, been turned into common property for a finite number of states, though not necessarily a small number. Then there are others that straddle into what is left of the high seas, and some are even wholly confined to the high seas. Fish stocks on the high seas used to be the prototype of open-access resources, with all their attendant problems discussed in Chapter 4. Whether or not that is still the case can be debated; stocks on the high seas are supposed to be managed by regional fisheries management organizations, but how forceful their writ is on the high seas is still uncertain; in any event, these organizations lack the authority and infrastructure to enforce their decisions. These matters are discussed in Chapter 6.

How likely is it that countries sharing a stock that migrates between their economic zones, and perhaps into the high seas as well, will manage them effectively? Some thoughts on this are offered in Chapter 7, drawing on game theory. Since sovereign states are involved, agreements have to be self-enforcing; that is, a country must find it in its interest to follow the agreement rather than go its own way. If countries do not cooperate and instead try to maximize their catches, or profits, in isolation, this will result in considerable losses even for the country itself, compared to what could be obtained under cooperation. Although countries could in many situations obtain a short-term gain by defecting from cooperation, or by refusing to cooperate, these gains would be transient and eroded by other countries acting in a similar fashion. Much depends on the far-sightedness of countries and how strongly they discount the future, as well as how diluted the losses from non-cooperation are. It is possible to construct scenarios in which the discount rate is so high and the losses from non-cooperation are spread among so many participants in a fishery that defection from cooperation would be profitable and thus destroy a cooperative agreement.

One issue that unavoidably arises in the context of migrating stocks is the division of catch quotas between the countries involved. A self-enforcing division of catch quotas is likely to favour small players, the reason being that they know that the big players have more at stake and will be willing to bear a disproportional conservation burden in their own interest. Small players can ride for free on such efforts. Two stocks with ample opportunities for free riding and a possibly severe decimation through competitive fishing are the Northeast Atlantic mackerel and the Norwegian spring-spawning herring.

The negotiations about catch quotas for these stocks among the countries concerned have quite frequently failed to produce an agreement involving all parties. These breakdowns in negotiations have usually been accompanied by forceful rhetoric about irresponsibility and disrespect for sustainable fishing. Yet, if one looks at the development of the stocks, it seems unaffected by this; periods with absence of comprehensive agreements have not produced more stock declines than periods with such agreements. It appears that the countries fishing these stocks in fact are engaged in an informal cooperation despite refusing to come to a formal agreement. Narrowly self-interested and myopic behaviour would undoubtedly have resulted in a much worse outcome.

Approaches to fisheries management

Chapter 8 deals with the approaches to fisheries management. Many stocks worldwide are now managed by individual fish quotas, even stocks that are shared by two or more countries. This way of managing shared stocks would not have happened without the 200-mile limit. Within that limit, coastal states can arrest boats that violate international agreements on fish quotas and other fisheries regulations and fine their captains and owners. Fisheries management by individual quotas has a lot to recommend itself, not least from an economic point of view. If individual quotas are made transferable, both in the long and the short run, they provide incentives to fish a given quantity at the lowest possible cost or to turn the fish into products of highest value. In particular, individual transferable quotas are the instrument of choice to deal with technological progress. This arrangement gives boat owners incentives to invest in boats of an appropriate size to take the amount of fish they can expect to take, and, should bigger boats become more economic to use, additional quotas can be purchased to provide a sufficient basis for a bigger boat. Needless to say, annual fish quotas will vary up and down according to the natural fluctuations in the fish stocks. Boatowners will have to make the best-informed forecast about what their quota allocations will allow them to take when making their investment decisions.

The main drawback of individual quotas is the cost of monitoring. In fisheries conducted by small craft landing their catches on the beach, individual fish quotas would be hopeless to implement. This is likely also to be the case in countries with widespread corruption. The best instrument under these circumstances is effort management, issuing licences to boats and regulating their fishing time. Counting boats and monitoring whether or not they are fishing is relatively straightforward, but the problem is the definition and measurement of fishing effort. One would want to regulate fishing mortality in order to keep the fish stocks at some preferred target, but the number of boats and their time at sea, even if corrected for boat size and other characteristics, is not necessarily proportional to the fishing mortality their activity produces. Under such management, technological progress is often perceived as a problem rather than an advantage; new boats may be much more effective than boats used to be, making it necessary to reduce the number of boats or restrict their use, with all the attendant acrimony, in order to keep the fish stocks reasonably plentiful. Chapter 8 ends with a short discussion of fisheries subsidies, a truly misplaced measure in fisheries policy.

Chapter 9 offers perspectives and conclusions. The most successful fisheries management would be market-driven and guided by sound scientific principles. A necessary management reform would seek to minimize influence by politicians and instead make fisheries management an autonomous institution, whereby fish quotas are set on a scientific basis and the industry is left to decide how fish quotas are caught and for what purpose. The stagnation in the capture fisheries and increasing reliance on terrestrial plants for fish feed indicates that food from the sea will not contribute much to increasing the food supply for the growing human population. For that to happen, a technological revolution would be needed – one that is difficult to foresee at this time.

2
WORLD FISHERIES: SOME BASIC FACTS

In this chapter, we shall discuss some basic facts about the fishing industry. How has fish production developed in recent times? What is its role in the supply of food in the world? How has the composition of its products changed? What is the structure of the fishing industry like? Are world fisheries in a crisis in the sense that the food sources of the oceans are being depleted? How large is international trade in fish products and what is the main direction of its flow? Are tariffs a substantial hindrance to this trade?

By "fishing industry", we primarily mean capture of fish in lakes or the oceans and the production of edible or useable material from these captures. But "fish is a fish is a fish", as it was once put in the title of an academic paper (Gordon, Salvanes & Atkins 1994). Fish and other aquatic organisms are also farmed, fenced in by pens floating in the water or in ponds or tanks on land. The capture-based fishing industry meets aquaculture in the market-place; both compete with similar products for the food budgets of consumers who often are indifferent to, or even ignorant about, where the goods they purchase come from: capture fisheries or aquaculture. When discussing fish markets and products and their trends it is difficult or impossible, and per-haps even pointless, to distinguish where the fish come from. Our discus-sion of fish production and trade will include farmed products, but otherwise this book is mainly concerned with the capture-based industry. Fish capture and fish farming are two very different activities; fish capture is essentially hunting with advanced equipment, but nevertheless subject to the vagaries of nature: variations in the weather and the availability or abundance of fish stocks. There is often high risk and uncertainty associated with this activity.

Fish farming has much in common with agriculture: the fish stocks are kept under control; broods of fish are put out, fed and slaughtered according to plan. Even so, fish farming has its own risks as a result of the variability of nature: rough weather may destroy fish pens and put the fish on the run; poisonous algae may develop, and parasites have a field day in fish pens, as always when animals are crowded together and fed indiscriminately. These matters will be discussed in greater detail in Chapter 3.

World production of fish

Figure 2.1 shows captures and total production of aquatic (marine and inland waters) organisms since 1950. The phrase "aquatic organisms" covers more than fish; it also includes plants (mainly seaweed), crustaceans (such as shrimp and prawns) and molluscs (clams, mussels, oysters, scallops, squids, octopuses, and more), but fish accounts for more than 80 per cent of the total in the capture fisheries. Seals and whales are not included, as their captures are often reported in numbers of animals and not weight, but they are a very small part of the total anyway.[1] The word "fish" is often used loosely to also include crustaceans and molluscs, and this will often be done in the following. From 1950 to 1970 the captures of fish (in the sense just mentioned) grew exponentially at a rate of about 6 per cent per year, from 18 to 60 million tonnes. After that growth slowed down, and since the mid-1990s the captures of fish have stagnated just below 100 million tonnes per year.

At this point it is appropriate to acknowledge that "captures" is a somewhat misleading term; the data record landings and not captures in a strict sense. A non-negligible amount of fish captured is thrown overboard because it is for some reason unwanted. The FAO has tried to estimate how much fish is discarded and never brought ashore. The most recent estimate is about 9 million tonnes per year from 2010 to 2014, which is about 10 per cent of the fish landed (see Pérez Roda *et al.* 2019). This is a lot less than reported in the first study, from the early 1990s, which estimated discards at 27 million tonnes per year, but with wide confidence limits (Alverson *et al.* 1996). Estimating discards is obviously prone to be imprecise, partly because discards are illegal in some countries. One reason why fish are discarded is that they may not be marketable; another is that dealing with different types of fish that require very different processing

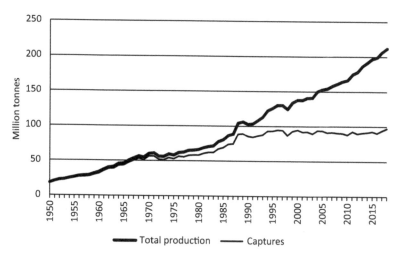

Figure 2.1 Captures and total production of aquatic organisms (excluding seals and whales, but including aquatic plants), 1950–2018
Source: Fishery Statistical Collection (FAO).

can be cumbersome and expensive. Much of the discards take place in shrimp fisheries, when other types of fish (shrimp are not even fish in a strict sense) are invariably caught together with the shrimp, but require different handling or are too small to be marketed (shrimps must be caught with nets with small meshes, which also sweep up small fish that cannot be marketed).

Despite the stagnation in the capture fisheries, the total production of aquatic organisms has continued to grow. The difference between total production and captures is due to aquaculture, which has grown from 3.6 million tonnes in 1970 to 115 million tonnes in 2018, at an annualized rate of over 7 per cent. Aquaculture thus has superseded captures of aquatic organisms in the wild, and it seems safe to say that any further increase in the production of such organisms will have to come from aquaculture. In the period from 1961 to 2017 the average annual increase in fish consumption (3.1 per cent) outpaced population growth (1.6 per cent per year) and exceeded the growth of consumption of meat from terrestrial animals (2.7 per cent per year). Only the consumption of poultry has grown more rapidly (4.7 per cent per year) than the consumption of fish (FAO 2020: 65).

Table 2.1 shows the top 20 producers of aquatic organisms (except whales and seals) from 2014 to 2018. China dwarfs everyone else, both in capture fisheries and aquaculture, being responsible for almost 40 per cent of world production. Indonesia and India rank as numbers 2 and 3, both in total and in capture fisheries and aquaculture. Some countries are mainly engaged in capture fisheries, others in aquaculture. Egypt is number 9 in aquaculture production but 46 in capture fisheries, and Morocco is number 18 in capture fisheries but 125 in aquaculture. The United States and Russia both rank high in capture fisheries, 4 versus 6, but only as 18 and 28 in aquaculture. For the United States this undoubtedly reflects the considerable opposition to aquaculture from environmental groups, while in Russia the reason probably is natural disadvantage, such as cold waters, inhospitable to farmed fish and other marine organisms. Peru is number 5 in capture fisheries, but only 38 in aquaculture. Peru is big in capture fisheries because of

Table 2.1 Average production (million tonnes) of aquatic organisms (excluding whales and seals) in the top 20 countries, 2014–18

Country	Total	Rank	Capture	Rank	Aquaculture	Rank
China	77.8	1	15.9	1	61.9	1
Indonesia	22.2	2	6.8	2	15.4	2
India	11.0	3	5.2	3	5.8	3
Vietnam	6.7	4	3.1	8	3.7	4
United States	5.4	5	4.9	4	0.4	18
Russia	4.9	6	4.7	6	0.2	28
Peru	4.8	7	4.7	5	0.1	38
Japan	4.4	8	3.4	7	1.1	11
Philippines	4.4	9	2.1	11	2.3	5
Bangladesh	3.9	10	1.7	13	2.2	6
Norway	3.8	11	2.5	9	1.3	8
South Korea	3.4	12	1.5	16	1.9	7
Chile	3.4	13	2.3	10	1.2	10
Myanmar	3.1	14	2.0	12	1.0	12
Thailand	2.5	15	1.6	14	0.9	13
Malaysia	1.9	16	1.5	17	0.5	17
Mexico	1.8	17	1.6	15	0.2	24
Egypt	1.7	18	0.4	46	1.3	9
Morocco	1.4	19	1.4	18	0.0	125
Brazil	1.3	20	0.7	26	0.6	15

Source: Fishery Statistical Collection (FAO).

the anchovy fishery, usually the biggest fishery in the world, but highly variable, as will be discussed later. Most of the anchovies are converted to meal
and oil and end up as feed for farmed fish (see Chapter 3), mainly exported
to other countries.

Is there a "crisis" in world fisheries?

Many people talk about the "crisis" in the world's capture fisheries, meaning
that the world oceans are rapidly being depleted because of overfishing. That
is not the picture staring us in the face from Figure 2.1; what we see is stagnation, not depletion. But below the aggregate picture lurk murkier stories. Some
types of fish and individual fish stocks have declined. Some have collapsed,
though all of these have recovered, at least partially. Total extinction of fish
species because of overfishing seems rare, and possibly non-existent; a recent
report by fisheries scientists puts it like this: "There is apparently no example
of species driven to extinction by fisheries, but numerous examples of extinction of exploited fish populations in which fishing might have been a factor"
(Garcia *et al.* 2018: 40).

The FAO has for some time published accounts of the status of select fish
stocks, and their reports are widely quoted. The most recent one is from
2020, where we find that the fraction of assessed stocks that are overfished
increased from 10 per cent in 1974 to 34 per cent in 2017 (FAO 2020: 47; for
methodology see FAO 2011). This points in the wrong direction. The share
of overfished stocks has changed little, however, for about ten years (FAO
2020: 48). About 60 per cent of all stocks were fully fished in 2017 – that is,
close to the maximum sustainable yield level – which is good news rather than
bad, from the point of view of providing food supplies. "Percentage of stocks"
makes no reference to landed quantity, but the FAO's latest report informs
us that almost 80 per cent of all fish landings in 2017 came from biologically
sustainable stocks (FAO 2020: 47).

In the following we shall look at how the catches from a few important
stocks have developed over time. At this point we need to note that increases
or decreases in fish catches do not necessarily indicate correctly how the fish
stock providing them is developing; such changes could be due to changes in
fishing activity. Still less do they necessarily indicate the degree of exploitation;

if the underlying fish stock is blooming because of advantageous environmental conditions, catches will increase even if the rate of exploitation does not change. But, if fish catches decline consistently over a long time despite no decline in fishing activity, one would certainly suspect that something is wrong about the underlying stock.

Figures 2.2 to 2.5 show the catches of four types of gadoid (cod-like) fishes from 1950 to 2018, popular staple food fishes in Europe and North America. The catches of Alaska pollock rose from almost nothing in 1950 to a peak of almost 7 million tonnes in 1988. The Japanese were the pioneers in developing this fishery; between 1972 and 1974 they caught about 3 million tonnes. In 1976 the United States established an exclusive national fisheries zone 200 miles wide, and a bit later the Soviet Union came along with a 200-mile exclusive economic zone. The Japanese could no longer fish in what had become American or Soviet waters except by agreement with those countries, and the Japanese catches duly declined while the American and Russian catches shot up. The sudden increase in Russian/Soviet catches from nothing to more than 3 million tonnes in 1988 looks suspicious, so if numbers for earlier years are missing the increase was more gradual than what we see in the figure. The Russian catches have declined substantially since the sudden peak in 1988 and have been comparable to the American ones since the beginning of this century.

After the Americans established their 200-mile zone, Americanization of the fishery in the US zone became a goal. The market developed rapidly, and a kind of "gold rush" set in. The American catches rose from nothing before 1975 to 1.4 million tonnes in 1988 and have been relatively stable after that. Realizing that uncontrolled access was not sustainable, the Americans set about regulating their fishery, and quota limits were put in place. The US fishery appears to be quite responsibly regulated; the annual catch has fluctuated only moderately and has trended upwards. Since the Alaska pollock is subject to substantial environmental variability just like any other type of fish, the Americans may in fact have forgone some benefits by not allowing larger catches in years when the fish stock has been in good shape. According to the Marine Stewardship Council, the Gulf of Alaska pollock fishery is "exceptionally well managed and ... characterized by state of the art stock assessments and harvest strategies. The stock is in a good condition" (quoted in Samró 2016: 154). There is another pollock fishery in Alaska, the

Figure 2.2 Catches of Alaska pollock, 1950–2018
Source: Fishery Statistical Collection (FAO).

Bering Sea/Aleutian Islands fishery, but there is reason to believe that the same is also valid in that case.

Catches of Atlantic cod (Figure 2.3) peaked in 1968 at just below 3 million tonnes and then trended down until 2008, when the catches were just 771,000 tonnes. Atlantic cod consists of several stocks (Northeast Arctic cod, Icelandic cod, Baltic cod, North Sea cod, Northern cod of Newfoundland, and more), all of which have had a somewhat different development. In Chapter 5 we shall discuss three of these in greater detail (Northeast Arctic cod, Icelandic cod and the Northern cod of Newfoundland). Cod has for a long time been an important fish in Western Europe, some Mediterranean countries and the northeast of North America.

European hake (Figure 2.4) is an important source of food in Spain and Portugal and several other countries. The catches of this fish trended downwards until the turn of the twenty-first century, from a peak of 167,000 tonnes in 1955 to a trough of 58,000 tonnes in 2001. The years after that have seen a rapid recovery; the catches from 2016 to 2018 were about 140,000 tonnes, a level not seen since 1975.

Atlantic cod

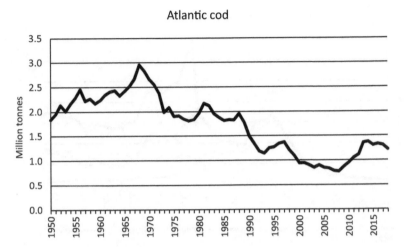

Figure 2.3 Catches of Atlantic cod, 1950–2018
Source: Fishery Statistical Collection (FAO).

European hake

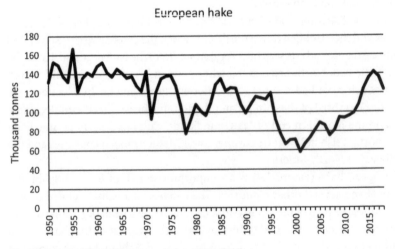

Figure 2.4 Catches of European hake, 1950–2018
Source: Fishery Statistical Collection (FAO).

Haddock is a popular staple fish in Britain, New England and many other countries around the North Atlantic. The catches of haddock reached a short-lived peak of over 700,000 tonnes in 1969 (Figure 2.5). After that they were on a declining trend to a trough of 200,000 in the early 1990s, but have trended slightly upwards after that. In terms of quantity, these four fish types are among the ten most important cod-like fishes, so classified in the FAO statistics. The development of catches from these stocks provide only limited support, if any, for the notion that we are depleting the food sources of the ocean; a declining trend has been reversed, and in some cases (European hake, Northeast Arctic cod) recovery has been substantial.

Herring and other pelagic fish (fish living close to the surface, as opposite to close to or on the bottom) are even more prone to fluctuations caused by environmental factors. These are often proxied by ocean temperature, but are probably related to variability in plankton supply (these fish feed on plankton, in contrast to gadoids, which feed mainly on other fish). We will look at some individual stocks in Chapter 5, where we discuss environmental fluctuations. In Figures 2.6 to 2.9 we look at the development of catches of four pelagic fish species, all of which display extreme variability in catches.

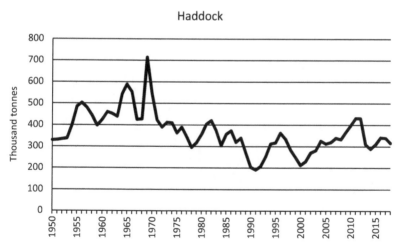

Figure 2.5 Catches of haddock, 1950–2018
Source: Fishery Statistical Collection (FAO).

The catches of Peruvian anchovy are shown in Figure 2.6. This fishery developed initially in response to the collapse of the California sardine catch (Figure 2.8). The California sardine supported major fishmeal and canning industries, which suddenly found themselves bereft of their raw material. The Peruvian fishing industry stepped into the void; some equipment was even shipped from California to Peru. The fishery grew rapidly to become the biggest in the world, reaching 13 million tonnes in 1970. Then, in 1972, came a strong El Niño event. This interfered with the food supply for the Peruvian anchovy, and the fishery collapsed to 170,000 tonnes in 1972. It continued at a low level and fell below 100,000 tonnes in 1984. It recovered after that and again overshot the 12 million mark in 1994. In 1997/98 a strong El Niño event occurred again, but the decline in catches was short-lived. Between 2014 and 2017 the catches were only 3 to 4 million tonnes, which is relatively little. In this period there was again an El Niño event. In 2018 the catches passed 7 million tonnes.

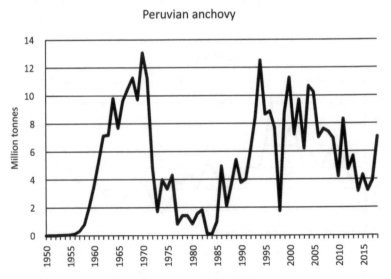

Figure 2.6 Catches of Peruvian anchovy, 1950–2018
Source: Fishery Statistical Collection (FAO).

Atlantic herring

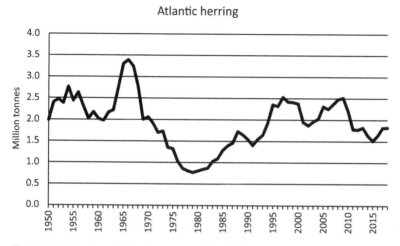

Figure 2.7 Catches of Atlantic herring, 1950–2018
Source: Fishery Statistical Collection (FAO).

Figure 2.7 shows the catches of Atlantic herring. They reached a peak of 3.4 million tonnes in 1966 and fell thereafter to a trough of 770,000 tonnes in 1979. The Atlantic herring population consists of several herring stocks, and this aggregate picture conceals the virtual collapse of individual stocks, such as the Norwegian spring-spawning herring in the late 1960s and the North Sea herring a few years later. We shall discuss the Norwegian spring-spawning herring in greater detail in Chapter 5. After 1980 the catches trended upwards, and since the mid-1990s they have varied around 2 million tonnes. The fluctuations around this level have been substantial, however.

The California sardine collapsed in the early 1950s and took with it the canning and meal industry in California (Figure 2.8). The catches remained low until the early 1970s. From the early 1980s they grew to a peak of 760,000 tonnes in 2009, but with substantial fluctuations. Then they plummeted to between 60,000 and 100,000 tonnes in the 2015–18 period. We shall return to the California sardine in Chapter 5.

Figure 2.9 shows the catches of the Japanese sardine; the graph displays a typical boom-bust pattern. The catches were very small in the years before 1973, below 100,000 tonnes. Then they rose suddenly to a peak of 5.4 million

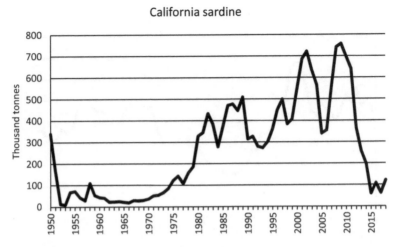

Figure 2.8 Catches of California sardine, 1950–2018
Source: Fishery Statistical Collection (FAO).

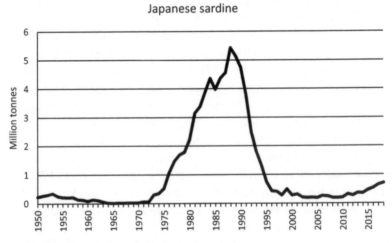

Figure 2.9 Catches of Japanese sardine, 1950–2018
Source: Fishery Statistical Collection (FAO).

tonnes in 1988, before falling precipitously to 430,000 tonnes in 1996. For years they hovered around 200,000 tonnes, but since 2010 they have slowly risen again. The driving force behind the rise and fall of the Japanese sardine is changes in ocean currents, reflected in changes in sea surface temperature (see Jang, Yamazaki & Hoshino 2019).

The extreme variability of the catches of these four pelagic stocks, and many other similar ones, are caused by the variability of the environment. Excessive fishing may accentuate these fluctuations, and could in the worst case lead to an annihilation of the stock, at least in commercial terms. We shall discuss this problem further in Chapter 5. It is not possible to stabilize the catches from such stocks except at ridiculously low levels, which would mean forgoing the benefits the "blooming" episodes of these stocks provide.

Bluefin tuna is probably the most pricy fish in the world. It is a sought-after ingredient in high-quality sushi, and the price is correspondingly high. Occasionally, astronomical prices are reported for bluefin tunas. The second highest reported to that date was in early January 2020, ¥193.2 million for a bluefin tuna of 276 kilogram (kg), which comes to more than US$6,000 per kilogram.

High market prices combined with lax control generate a pressure for deple-tion, as will be discussed in Chapter 4. This scenario is particularly likely to play out for fish stocks caught in international waters or that migrate between the economic zones of different countries, an issue that will be discussed in Chapters 6 and 7. Yet we do not see any strong indication of this happening for the bluefin tuna. Figure 2.10 shows the catches since 1950 for the three bluefin tuna stocks in the world. The catches from all three vary a great deal, as is true for most, if not all, other fish stocks, but there is little or no trend in the catches for two of them, the Pacific and the Atlantic bluefin. The catches of Southern bluefin tuna, which is caught in the Indian Ocean, have declined severely since a peak of over 80,000 tonnes in 1961, but since 1990 the catches have varied without trend between 10,000 and 20,000 tonnes. Even for the supposedly vulnerable bluefin tuna the alleged fishery crisis is not clearly visible.

We end this discussion of fish stocks with the orange roughy, a fishery that began as late as 1979 (Figure 2.11). This is a deep-water fish caught by bottom trawls at depths of 800 to 1,300 metres (Tingley & Dunn 2018: 4). Like many other fish living in cold and deep waters, the orange roughy grows very slowly and is believed to have a lifespan of decades, with some specimens being more

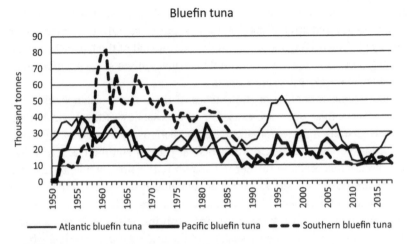

Figure 2.10 Catches of bluefin tuna, 1950–2018
Source: Fishery Statistical Collection (FAO).

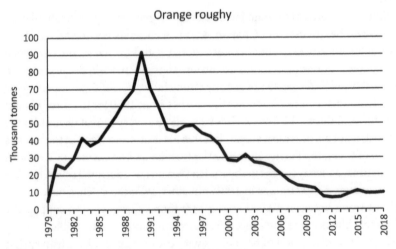

Figure 2.11 Catches of orange roughy, 1979–2018
Source: Fishery Statistical Collection (FAO).

than 100 years old. When concerns arose about the sustainability of this fishery, some campaign groups hatched the slogan "Would you eat a fish that is older than your grandmother?".

The fishery began in the waters off New Zealand and is still largely conducted there, even if orange roughy have been discovered elsewhere, including the Atlantic Ocean. It developed very quickly; catches rose from 5,000 tonnes in 1979 to over 90,000 tonnes in 1990. Then they fell almost as rapidly as they had risen before, to 7,400 tonnes in 2011, and have since been about 10,000 tonnes per year.

Two factors explain the development of the catches of orange roughy over time. First, the fishery began with a pristine stock in the late 1970s. For slow-growing stocks, the standing stock is very large compared with the sustainable catches that can be taken from the stocks. Therefore, there will be an initial phase of large, unsustainable catches as the stock is driven down from a pristine equilibrium to a new one producing a sustainable yield (we shall explain these concepts in greater detail in Chapter 4). So, what we are seeing in Figure 2.11 is the "mining" phase, when a stock is driven down with unsustainable catches to a new equilibrium. Second, very little was known initially about the life history of the orange roughy, and fisheries scientists in New Zealand and elsewhere overestimated the sustainable yield of the stock. The permitted catches from the stock were probably excessive until a better assessment of the yield potential of the stock became available, which contributed to the sharp peak we see in Figure 2.11.[2]

Fishery products and their role in world food supplies

Figure 2.12 shows the changes in the composition of fish products since 1976. Two things are particularly noteworthy. First, the share of fresh, chilled or frozen fish has almost doubled, from 31 per cent in 1976 to 55 per cent in 2017. We also see a similar development for crustaceans and molluscs. This is attributable to improvements in transportation and freezing or cooling technology; in most cases fresh fish is preferred over preparations such as salted, dried or canned, though some such preparations undoubtedly have produced their own acquired taste. Canning, salting and drying have given some ground, though the latter two have held up better than one might

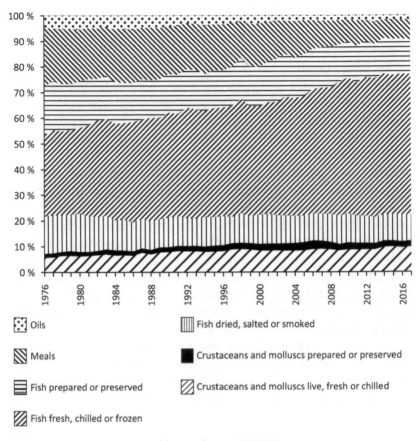

Oils

Meals

Fish prepared or preserved

Fish fresh, chilled or frozen

Fish dried, salted or smoked

Crustaceans and molluscs prepared or preserved

Crustaceans and molluscs live, fresh or chilled

Figure 2.12 Major categories of fish products, 1976–2017
Source: Fishery Statistical Collection (FAO).

expect and owe their continued existence to old traditions that trump long distances. Dried cod and salted dried cod have strong traditional markets in the Catholic countries of southern Europe and their offspring in Latin America. In the Norwegian export statistics for 2018 we find, for example, that Portugal was the number one recipient (61 per cent by value) of dried salted cod from Norway, followed by Brazil (18 per cent). For dried cod not salted from the Lofoten Islands we find Italy dominating, with 75 per cent, followed by Croatia, the United States and Nigeria, with about 6 per cent each. These products are hardly consumed in Norway itself, nor in any of the neighbouring countries. Fish on Fridays and during Lent has a long history. Salting and drying were necessary to preserve the fish and transport them over long distances before freezing technology was developed. Drying cod in open air without salting it first is a method that dates from before Viking times and was due to the traditional scarcity of salt. This product was the main speciality of the Hanseatic outpost in Bergen for hundreds of years from the fourteenth century onwards.

The other main change to note from Figure 2.12 is the relative decline in the production of fishmeal and fish oil (the absolute level of production has been stagnant for a decade or more). These products used to be mixed with other feedstuff in feed blends for pigs and poultry and have desirable properties for the growth of these animals. As fish farming increased, it demanded more and more fishmeal and fish oil, and is now the main recipient of these products, though they are still used in feed for terrestrial animals. The feed demands of the fish-farming industry have long since outstripped the capacity of the fishmeal industry, as will be discussed in the next chapter.

What is the role of fish in the food supply of the world? The FAO has for years calculated the contribution of various food products to the food supply of the world. In 2017, 7 per cent of world protein supplies and 17 per cent of animal protein came from fish, shares that have not changed much for decades (FAO 2020: 67). But there are wide differences between countries. On top is the British Virgin Islands, with nearly 60 per cent of the protein supplies coming from fish.[3] Well below come island states such as the Maldives (about 50 per cent), the Faeroe Islands (27 per cent) and Iceland (20 per cent). The Pacific island states also get 20 per cent or more of their protein supplied from fish. Japan, a fish-eating country of renown, is just below 20 per cent. Several mainly landlocked states get less than 1 per cent of their protein from fish (Afghanistan, Uzbekistan, Tajikistan, Azerbaijan, Mongolia, Syria, Eritrea, Ethiopia, Guinea-Bissau, Lesotho, Niger). Surprisingly, we find an island, Puerto Rico, in this latter category, and it is a neighbour to the British Virgin Islands with the highest share of protein supplies coming from fish.

There are other ways of putting the seafood industry into perspective. Figure 2.13 compares supplies of world food from fish and other marine and

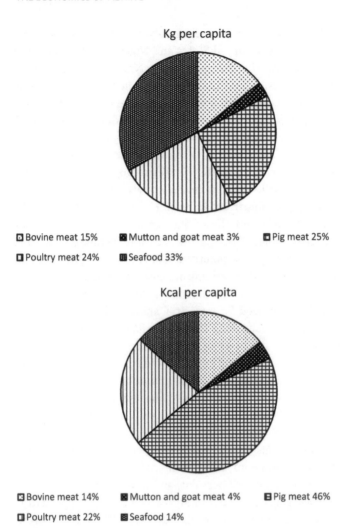

Kg per capita

- ◘ Bovine meat 15%
- ▓ Mutton and goat meat 3%
- ▣ Pig meat 25%
- ▢ Poultry meat 24%
- ▦ Seafood 33%

Kcal per capita

- ◙ Bovine meat 14%
- ▓ Mutton and goat meat 4%
- ▤ Pig meat 46%
- ▥ Poultry meat 22%
- ▦ Seafood 14%

Figure 2.13 World food supply from seafood and meats from land animals, 2017
Source: FAOSTAT: "New food balances".

freshwater organisms with supplies of bovine and pig meat, poultry meat, and mutton and goat meat. It matters quite a bit whether we make these comparisons in weight per capita or in kilocalories per capita. If we go for weight per capita, we find that seafood is considerably more important than both poultry and pig meat, accounting for about one-third of the total. In this comparison, pig and poultry are well behind seafood, and bovine meat well behind those two again. If, on the other hand, we look at kilocalories per capita, we find that seafood is comparable to bovine meat, with each responsible for 14 per cent of the total, while pig meat accounts for almost a half of the calories from all four. Seafood is relatively rich in protein content but poor in terms of energy (measured in calories).

Table 2.2 shows the consumption per capita of fish in the top versus bottom 25 countries and jurisdictions. Much is as expected, but there are a few

Table 2.2 Fish consumption (kilograms live weight) per capita in top versus bottom 25 countries and jurisdictions, 2016

Top 25			*Bottom 25*		
1	Maldives	142.3	1	Afghanistan	0.2
2	Iceland	91.3	2=3	Puerto Rico	0.4
3	Greenland	87.8	2=3	Tajikistan	0.4
4	Faeroe Islands	87.5	4=5	Ethiopia	0.5
5	St Helena	74.9	4=5	Mongolia	0.5
6	Cook Islands	72.0	6	Eritrea	0.8
7	Wallis and Futuna	71.4	7	Sudan	1.1
8	Kiribati	68.0	8	Guinea-Bissau	1.3
9	Palau	59.5	9	Syria	1.5
10	Seychelles	58.3	10	Lesotho	1.7
11	Portugal	57.1	11	Pakistan	1.8
12	South Korea	56.5	12	Niger	2.1
13	Norway	50.0	13	Somalia	2.2
14	Antigua and Barbuda	49.7	14	Uzbekistan	2.3
15	Singapore	49.1	15	Kyrgyzstan	2.4
16	Myanmar	47.8	16	Burundi	2.5
17	Spain	47.7	17=18	Bolivia	2.6
18	Bermuda	47.6	17=18	Iraq	2.6
19	French Polynesia	47.4	19	Guatemala	2.6
20	Samoa	47.3	20=22	Palestine	2.7
21	Aruba	47.0	20=22	Nepal	2.7
22	Turks and Caicos Islands	46.5	20=22	Azerbaijan	2.7
23	Anguilla	46.3	23	South Sudan	2.9
24	Nauru	46.1	24	Eswatini (Swaziland)	3.1
25	Japan	45.3	25	Reunion	3.2

Source: (FAO 2019).

surprises. The Maldives hold the record by far, with more than 140 kg, with the North Atlantic island states of Iceland, Greenland and the Faeroe Islands following, with around 90 kg. The top ten are all islands. Then follow three countries with a long coastline, Portugal, South Korea and Norway, with Spain not far behind. Japan is number 25, with a consumption of 45 kg per capita. For comparison, the United States and Canada consume a half of that, 22 kg per capita, and the United Kingdom 20 kg. The bottom fish eaters are mainly land-locked states, but there are a few surprises: Puerto Rico (number two from the bottom) has been mentioned; Guinea-Bissau is a coastal country; and Reunion is an island.

International trade in fish

Fish products are widely traded. According to the FAO, they are some of the most traded food items in the world today (FAO 2018: 52). In 2017 the total exports of fish, crustaceans and molluscs amounted to US$158 billion (FAO Fisheries Statistical Collection). This is more than the total exports of meat (US$144 billion in 2017) or beverages and tobacco (US$147 billion in 2017) (FAOSTAT database). Poor countries export more fish to rich countries than the other way around. Table 2.3 shows exports less imports of fish, crustaceans and molluscs in 2017. We see that rich countries had a deficit of US$31.5 billion while developing countries had a surplus of US$41.3 billion. The export and import figures do not match; there is a discrepancy of US$9.8 billion.

Some of the export surplus of developing countries is attributable to the fact that rich countries export some of their fish catches to developing countries for processing, in order to take advantage of low wages, and then import the finished product. Because processing adds value, this will generate an excess

Table 2.3 Exports less imports of fish, crustaceans and molluscs (billion US dollars), 2017

Developed countries or areas	−31.5
Least developed countries	2.4
Other developing countries or areas	38.9
Sum	9.8

Source: Fishery Statistical Collection (FAO).

of exports over imports for the developing countries involved. Concerns have been raised that excess exports from developing countries generate a food deficit in countries with precarious food supplies, as poor countries will be exporting their food instead of using it at home. This has been investigated in at least two publications, which reach somewhat different conclusions. John Kurien, the author of the FAO report (FAO 2005), finds that fish exports from developing countries in most cases improved food security. A study by the WorldFish Center (WorldFish Center 2011) is less clear in its conclusions, however. Fish exports could improve a country's food supply, because high-value fish could finance imports of a larger volume of cheaper food, be it fish or other foodstuff.

Tariff barriers vary, but may perhaps be considered as relatively low for fish products; the FAO characterizes tariffs on fish products as "rather low", presumably by comparison to tariffs on agricultural products (FAO 2018: 57). The United States has no tariffs on most fish products. The European Union is less liberal; although it has trade agreements with several countries, it applies significant tariffs to those that are not included in such agreements. These tariffs are usually 12 to 20 per cent of the value. The EU tariffs are often differentiated according to the degree of processing; for example, the tariff on fresh salmon is 2 per cent while the tariff on smoked salmon is 13 per cent. This provides protection for the processing industry of the EU countries. Tariffs applied by other countries, developing and developed ones alike, vary a great deal, from zero in many cases to 20 to 30 per cent of value. Japan, a major fish importer, applies a tariff of 10 per cent for many fish products, but less, sometimes just 1 per cent, on others. China has a tariff of 7 per cent on most products, but both higher and lower rates on the rest.

Table 2.4 shows the top 20 importing and exporting countries in terms of value. China, the biggest producer by far, is also the biggest exporter by far. Norway is number two, even if it comes way further down the rank in terms of quantity produced (see Table 2.1). This is partly because Norway has a small home market and partly because it exports high-value products (salmon in particular). China is also a large importer; it ranks as number three on the list of importers. Many other countries also appear on both lists; the United States is the biggest importer of fish in the world, and it is also the fifth largest exporter. Russia imports almost as much fish in terms of value as it exports. The United Kingdom, Canada,

Table 2.4 Top 20 exporting and importing countries of aquatic products (billion US dollars), average 2013–17

Exports			Imports		
1	China	20.37	1	United States	20.67
2	Norway	10.51	2	Japan	14.84
3	Vietnam	7.53	3	China	9.21
4	Thailand	6.28	4	Spain	7.04
5	United States	5.81	5	France	6.41
6	India	5.57	6	Italy	6.06
7	Chile	5.53	7	Germany	5.64
8	Canada	4.77	8	Sweden	4.77
9	Denmark	4.67	9	South Korea	4.43
10	Spain	4.15	10	United Kingdom	4.35
11	Netherlands	4.14	11	Hong Kong SAR	3.69
12	Indonesia	4.13	12	Denmark	3.61
13	Ecuador	4.02	13	Netherlands	3.53
14	Sweden	3.95	14	Thailand	3.11
15	Russia	3.90	15	Canada	2.89
16	Germany	3.00	16	Russia	2.37
17	United Kingdom	2.79	17	Belgium	2.21
18	Peru	2.63	18	Poland	2.11
19	Iceland	2.12	19	Portugal	2.10
20	Morocco	2.07	20	Australia	1.62

Source: Fishery Statistical Collection (FAO).

Thailand, Denmark and Germany all appear on both lists. One explanation is variety: countries that catch a lot of fish of one particular kind export some of it and import other types that they do not produce themselves. Some countries import fish for further processing and export the final product; this is true of both China and Denmark, for example, both of which have a thriving fish-processing industry. As far as China and other developing countries are concerned, the reason for fish imports for processing is low labour costs, whereas for Denmark and other rich countries in a similar situation the reason most likely is technological know-how and better access to markets. Denmark, for example, imports fresh salmon from Norway for further processing because it is inside the EU tariff barrier, while Norway is outside as far as fish and agricultural products are concerned.

The fishing industry

It is difficult to generalize about the structure of the fishing industry. Fishing is conducted by a great variety of fishing equipment, from simple nets thrown from the beach and hand lines with a hook on one end to large high-tech vessels equipped with nets as large as a football field and fish-finding equipment able to detect shoals of fish in the water. Likewise, the boats cover the whole range from canoes made from tree trunks to ocean-going ships over 60 metres long and spacious enough to process the catch on board and store it for weeks if not months. A few numbers may illustrate the diversity. The FAO estimates that there were 4.6 million fishing boats in the world in 2018. Of these, 2.9 million were equipped with an engine. Of these again, 82 per cent were shorter than 12 metres and mostly undecked. The number of motorized boats over 24 metres long (roughly more than 100 gross tonnes) was estimated at 67,800 for 2018 (FAO 2020: 41–7).[4] The industry comprises everything from single-person operations to large, vertically integrated firms with their own fleets of big boats, some with operations virtually all over the globe. One such is the Spanish Nueva Pescanova, established after its predecessor Pescanova went through restructuring in 2015. The company has over 10,000 people employed on four continents and operates 70 boats, mostly in the Southern Hemisphere.

The type of technology to apply depends on the location and the behaviour of the fish. Small boats cannot go too far out, and they cannot deliver their catches in markets far from where the fish are caught. Fish accessible only far offshore require large boats beyond the means of an individual fisherman. Supplying customers who buy their food from supermarkets in urban areas requires a well-organized supply line. Not only is the handling and preservation technology demanding, modern ideas about traceability and transparent processes require a sophisticated organization beyond the means of the individual fisherman; only vertically integrated companies beyond a certain size can deal with these issues satisfactorily. This applies in equal measure to fish farming: the salmon fish-farming industry began on a small, experimental scale, but is now dominated by a few large firms with operations in many countries. An "old man and the sea" nostalgia may be appealing and quite satisfactory in local markets, where people can walk to the shore and buy their fish for the day, but it falls short of the demands of modern society, with its high degree of specialization, requiring long chains of preservation, transportation and traceability. There are now organizations such as the Marine Stewardship Council specializing in certifying that the fish supermarkets buy are caught legally and in conformity with environmental rules and regulations. This requires counterparts with sufficient muscle, such as government fisheries management bodies and firms of some critical size. Firms without a certificate from the Marine Stewardship Council, or any other of a similar kind, are likely to find themselves at a disadvantage when they try to sell their products to supermarket chains.

Even if there are many large seafood companies in the world, it would be a stretch to say that the world seafood industry is dominated by such companies, and certainly not if we compare with the petroleum industry, for example. The 100 largest seafood companies in the world had a revenue of US$100 billion in 2017.[5] Such a number means little unless it is related to something, but that "something" is elusive; there are no statistics readily available on the value produced worldwide by the seafood industry. The FAO has estimated the first-hand value in world fisheries and aquaculture in 2018 at about US$400 billion (FAO 2020: 2). The revenues of the largest 100 are about a quarter of that, but this certainly overstates their share of the world seafood market, for two reasons. First, processing and marketing, which are included in the revenues of the 100 firms, add a lot of value. Second, the large seafood companies are often engaged in other types of production, even the production of other types of food. The world market share of the top 100 is likely, therefore, to be much lower than a quarter. We can safely say that the world fishing industry includes a myriad of firms, large and small.

Henrik Österblom et al. (2015) made a comprehensive study of the 160 largest seafood companies in 2012 and preceding years. Interestingly, the top five companies in 2012 were the same as in 2017. They estimate that the 13 largest seafood companies handle 11 to 20 per cent of the total world catch in capture fisheries, but much more, 19 to 40 per cent, of the most valuable fisheries. They also discuss the influence of the large seafood companies in national and international management fora and acknowledge that this could improve management practices. Large companies are not interested in the erosion of their resource base or their reputation, or anything else that would diminish their ability to make money.

Of the 100 largest seafood companies, no fewer than 22 are located in Japan, but many of them operate in several countries around the world. This is perhaps not surprising: fish plays a large role in the Japanese diet, and Japan is one of the main fishing countries in the world, ranking as number eight for captured fish and seven for aquaculture (see Table 2.1). In the United States there are 13, in Norway nine and in China, Chile and Spain six each. The rest are spread across many countries with one, two or three in each.

The largest five of these 100 companies are Maruha Nichiro and Nippon Suisan Kaisha, both Japanese; Dongwon Enterprise, in South Korea; Mowi, in Norway; and the Thai Union Group, in Thailand. All of these, except Mowi, are conglomerates operating in many countries, both in fishing and aquaculture, and they also sell their products in many different countries. All those four are vertically integrated, either owning their fishing operations or shares in fishing companies. All four are engaged in acquisitions to strengthen their position either in the markets or in the fishing and processing operations leading to the final product. All four claim to operate on the basis of best practice and sustainability and have obtained certification from the Marine Stewardship Council or some other outfit engaged in issuing certificates of good environmental conduct. This is also true of many companies further down the list; they typically report sustainable fishing, backed by environmental certificates, and acquisitions of other companies in order to strengthen their position either in the consumer market or with respect to ensuring supplies. There is reason to believe that a further concentration of the seafood industry will take place, even if it would be wrong to characterize it as being dominated by just a few global companies so far.

Let us take a look at the biggest five, as they present themselves through their websites. Maruha Nichiro reports sales of about ¥900 billion per year in the period from 2016 to 2019, approximately US$8 billion. The company is also involved in selling food products other than seafood. It is active in the United States, Australia, New Zealand, Micronesia, Peru, Bangladesh, China, South Korea, Thailand, the Netherlands, the United Kingdom, South Africa and Namibia besides Japan itself. It has purchased shares in some of the fishing companies providing its raw material. Besides fishing, the company is engaged in aquaculture, raising amberjack, sea cucumber, yellowtail and bluefin tuna. The company has for years been engaged in research to hatch the eggs of bluefin tuna (farmed tuna are otherwise juveniles put in holding pens for fattening) and reports having achieved the first full-scale commercial shipping of egg-to-harvest tuna in 2016. The company is engaged in fishing in Alaska and claims a North American market share (2019) of 27 per cent for Alaska pollock, 30 per cent for crab and 12 per cent for salmon. In 2013 Maruha Nichiro acquired Seafood Connection, a Dutch company that purchases, processes and sells marine products. The accomplishments in Europe of this company are characterized as impressive; it has the largest market share of *Pangasius* (Mekong giant catfish) fillets.

Nippon Suisan Kaisha had sales of about ¥700 billion in 2018, a little over US$6 billion. The company claims to be one of the top ten producers in the US seafood industry. The company owns Salmones Antarctica in Chile, which is engaged in salmon aquaculture; EMDEPES, also in Chile, engaged in fishing; PESPASA in Argentina, also a fishing company; NAL Peru, which is responsible for the procurement of fishmeal and fish oil; and half of Sealord, a large fishing company in New Zealand. It owns marketing companies in Denmark (Nordic Seafood), the United States (Bryce) and Brazil (Nordsee). The company has processing bases in China, Taiwan, Vietnam and Thailand.

Dongwon is also engaged in other things than fishing or aquaculture (farming, for example). The company has acquired StarKist, an American tuna company with a well-known brand. Dongwon has interests in many countries across the globe. SCASA is a tuna manufacturer with an annual production capacity of 50,000 tonnes. SNCDS, the forerunner of SCASA, was the first canned tuna company in Africa and a government-owned one. It joined the Dongwon Group in 2011. Talofa Systems supplies high-quality materials for tuna can packaging to StarKist, the leading company of processed tuna in the United States. As the largest flexible packing materials company in Vietnam, TTP aims to expand the local market based on outstanding production cost competitiveness. It is dedicated to exports to enter overseas markets including Southeast Asia, using its growth in Vietnam as a foundation. CAPSEN is a Senegalese fishing company acquired by Dongwon. It started with one purse seine fishing vessel in 2015 and had four in 2018. Dongwon claims that it has grown into Senegal's best fishing company through partnership with the government.

Thai Union had total sales between 2015 and 2019 of about 130 billion baht per year – almost US$4 billion. It began as a canned tuna processor and exporter and is still mainly a processing and marketing company with its own brands. Its markets are all over the world: North America, Europe, Asia, and the Pacific.

Mowi, which ranks as number four, is different from the other top five in being a salmon aquaculture company. In 2018 its sales amounted to €3.8 billion, or US$4.5 billion. Mowi is the largest producer of farmed Atlantic salmon, with salmon farms in Norway, Chile, Scotland, Ireland, Canada and the Faeroe Islands. No less than 99 per cent of the Norwegian production is exported. Unlike the other top five, Mowi sells very little of its production in retail outlets under its own brand.

Looking at companies further down the list, we find stories not dissimilar to the five above. Some companies originated as processing and marketing companies with their own brands and still predominantly remain such, but have increasingly acquired stakes in fishing companies to ensure control over the whole supply chain. They have acquired environmental certifications for their operations from organizations such as the Marine Stewardship Council. They probably do this to get better access to retail chains that want to stay out of trouble in case their customers worry about the origins of the fish products they sell – whether they are sourced from fish stocks used sustainably or caught by methods that do not harm iconic animals such as sea birds or marine mammals. Some large seafood companies have evolved in the opposite direction, from fish capture companies to vertically integrated ones with their own processing plants and brands. Companies further down the list, such as the American Trident Seafood, the largest American seafood company, and the Icelandic Samherji, come to mind. Both started as one man (or, more accurately, a few men) with a boat, evolving over a couple of decades or so into large, vertically integrated companies with a whole fleet of boats, fish-processing plants and their own brand, with operations in many countries, in Samherji's case, and all over the United States, in Trident's case. Then there are a number of large, vertically integrated companies like Mowi, specializing in salmon farming, and quite a few companies involved both in fishing and fish farming.

Notes

1. Some molluscs are also reported in numbers and are not included.
2. Recently the FAO has published a comprehensive report on the orange roughy fisheries and their sustainability (Tingley & Dunn 2018).
3. This and the other numbers in this paragraph are from the FAO yearbook *Fisheries and Aquaculture Statistics 2017* (FAO 2019) and refer to 2016.
4. There is considerable uncertainty about these numbers, because not all countries report number of boats by length class.
5. This information is gathered by *Undercurrent News*, here quoted from Einarsson & Óladóttir (2020).

3

AQUACULTURE

As we have seen, the continued growth in production of aquatic organisms since the mid-1990s is due to aquaculture. Figure 3.1 shows the development of aquaculture production since 1970. The product mix of aquaculture is quite different, however, from capture fisheries. Fish, in the strict sense of the word, is barely one-half of the biomass produced by aquaculture (47 per cent in 2018). The largest category by weight is freshwater fish (40 per cent in 2018). Aquatic plants, mostly seaweed but also some microalgae, are the second largest category by weight: almost 30 per cent of the total production in 2018. Molluscs – that is, shellfish of various kinds (mussels, oysters, scallops, etc.) – rank as third, with 15 per cent in 2018. Then there are crustaceans, mainly shrimps, prawns, crawfish and crabs (8 per cent in 2018); diadromous fish, which include salmon (about 5 per cent in 2018); and marine fish (less than 3 per cent in 2018). In the capture fisheries (in a wide sense of the word), marine fish account for more than 70 per cent, freshwater fish for 11 per cent and aquatic plants for less than 1 per cent (numbers from 2018).

A rather different picture emerges if we look at value instead of quantity (Figure 3.2). Freshwater fish, crustaceans, molluscs and diadromous fish all have a higher value than aquatic plants, which have low value per unit weight; in 2018 they accounted for almost 30 per cent by weight but only 5 per cent by value, about the same as marine fish.

What are the species making up these broad categories? This is shown in Figure 3.3. Almost all cultivation of aquatic plants (not shown in the figure) takes place in four Asian countries: China, Indonesia, the Philippines and South Korea. Most of this is brown and red seaweed. Some is used for direct human consumption while the rest is a source of carrageenan, used by the

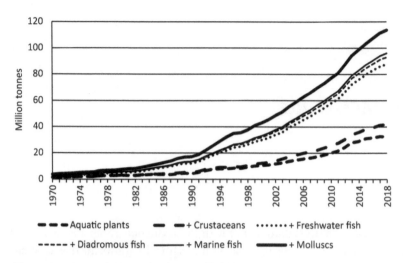

Figure 3.1 Aquaculture production, 1970–2018

Note: a small residual category (less than 1 million tonnes in 2018) is not shown.

Source: Fishery Statistical Collection (FAO).

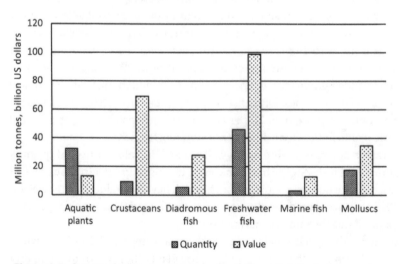

Figure 3.2 Quantity (million tonnes) and value (billion US dollars) of aquaculture organisms, 2018

Source: Fishery Statistical Collection (FAO).

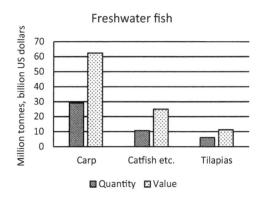

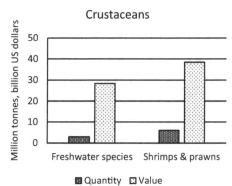

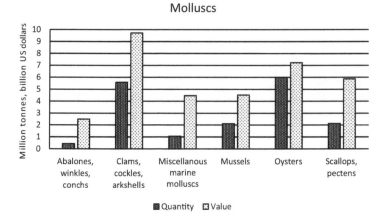

Figure 3.3 continued on next page

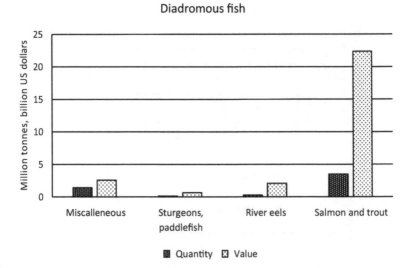

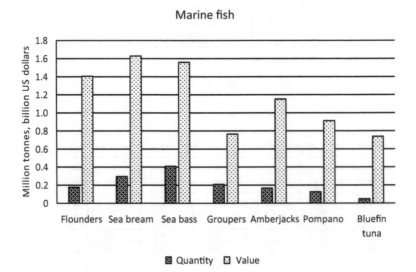

Figure 3.3 Quantity (million tonnes) and value (billion US dollars) of select aquaculture species, 2018
Source: Fishery Statistical Collection (FAO).

food industry as thickener and stabilizer. Freshwater fish consist of carps, tilapias and miscellaneous fish; the last category includes catfish, which some developing countries (Vietnam, for example) export to Europe and the United States. Catfish are also cultivated in the southern states of the United States. Carp cultivation has a long history; in medieval times monks cultivated carp, which forage their own food in ponds and can also be fed on scraps of various kinds.

Freshwater species, as well as shrimps and prawns, account for almost all of the production value of crustaceans, shrimps and prawns being more important.[1] Several types of molluscs are cultivated; the six types shown in the figure account for 99 per cent (2018) of the value of production. Clams, oysters and scallops are the most important in terms of value.

Most of the diadromous fish consist of salmon and trout, almost 90 per cent of value in 2018, but there is also some cultivation of river eels and sturgeons. The latter are very valuable, especially their eggs (caviar). The last category, marine fish, is extremely varied, and the species shown in the figure cover only 63 per cent by value (2018). Sea bream, sea bass and flounders (including soles and halibut) are the three most valuable species and have a reputation as high-quality fish in the rich countries of the world. It may be noted that bluefin tuna is number seven in the diagram in terms of value, but the value column is disproportionately high, because this is a very valuable fish. The culture of bluefin tuna means catching live juveniles and putting them in pens for fattening. As mentioned in Chapter 2, the Japanese conglomerate Maruha Nichiro has, after research over many years, managed to raise bluefin tuna from the egg stadium to a commercial-size fish and reported a first full-scale commercial shipping of egg-to-harvest tuna in 2016. The cultivation of some other marine fish, such as cod, also means catching live fish and putting them in pens for further gain in weight.

Aquaculture versus capture fisheries

As already mentioned, aquaculture is fundamentally different from capture fisheries, but both supply similar products to the same markets; fish consumers are often not even aware of whether the fish they buy is captured in the wild or comes from a fish farm. Those who are aware of the distinction often express a preference for the wild-captured fish, believing that their habitat is less affected by chemicals, used in fish feed or in treatment against diseases, or other contamination associated with fish farming. That may be so, but farmed fish have the advantage that the time from the slaughtering of the fish to the dinner table is often shorter than for wild fish, and all stages of this journey, especially the first ones, are under better control in aquaculture. It may take a long time for wild-captured fish to reach the fresh fish market or the pro-cessing plant, which can be a major disadvantage, because fish deteriorate quickly unless they are cleaned immediately and kept at low temperature. Fishing boats must steam to and from the fishing banks, which takes time. The fish are perhaps not exactly where they are supposed to be and the boats may spend considerable time filling up. On-board freezing has made it possible to preserve the freshness of the product, but, for farmed fish, these processes are much more tightly controlled.

The essential difference between fish farming and capture fisheries is the same as between farming and hunting. Fishing is essentially a form of hunting, often with impressive modern technology, but with a limited guarantee that a suitable concentration of fish will be found when and where the fishing firms, or fishermen, expect. The handling of the catch once on board is constrained by the limited space a fishing boat offers, even if it is highly impressive what boat designers have managed to do under the constraints they face. By con-trast, fish farming is much like animal husbandry. An aquaculture company cultivates its own eggs or buys them (or small, hatched fish) from another company, puts them into its holding pens, feeds them until they reach a suit-able size[2] and then ships them off to the market. The slaughtering of the fish can be planned almost to the day when the fish are wanted on the market, allowing for time of transportation, and the facilities where slaughtering and gutting take place are typically not constrained in space; there is usually enough space for whatever suitable facilities might be wanted in the vicinity of the fish farms.

The technologies and locations of fish farms vary from place to place and species to species. Often these are just dug-out ponds, suitable for catfish and carp, for example. In other cases, pens that float in the sea are used. This is the way salmon and trout are farmed. Farms with dug-out ponds place them on their own land or rented land, and their command over their facilities is as complete as private ownership or a lease contract allows. That said, the use of such private land, like all land use, is subject to environmental regulation necessitated by water contamination, which may happen in the fish ponds and cause damage to the public or to adjacent properties. Farms in floating pens are typically outside the bounds of any private property. Authorization by public authorities is necessary to establish such facilities, even if the adjacent land is privately owned. Each jurisdiction has its own rules about how facilities can be set up and run in the waters beyond the low water mark.[3]

In the following chapters, much of the discussion of capture fisheries will revolve around the fact that they take place in common waters beyond the property claims of anyone, exploiting fish stocks that also are common and not owned by any individual or firm. The fish-farming industry is much different from that arrangement. Fish farms own their fish stocks, feed them and decide when to slaughter them. Nevertheless, we encounter the common property problem in the cases when fish cages are placed in waters beyond the low water mark. These waters are common property in so far as they are used by many individuals for transportation and recreation. Some regulation is obviously necessary to avoid collisions between farming interests and transportational or recreational interests. Furthermore, diseases or contamination from feed or chemical spills may easily spill over to other fish farms in the vicinity, more so than between fish ponds on land, as such things travel more easily in water than through the soil. Therefore, regulations are necessary with respect to distances between fish farms or what to do in case a contiguous disease breaks out. There is thus some, albeit weak, similarity between capture fisheries exploiting common fish stocks and fish farms located in common waters.

Otherwise, the fish farmer has as full control over his fish stock as nature allows, much as a farmer has over their herd of pigs or cattle. But nature poses some risks to the fish farmer, just as it does to the animal farmer. Diseases have a field day where there are concentrations of animals in a confined place, be it swine in the pigsty or salmon in a pen, though the diseases are of course different. Diseases probably spread more quickly in water than they would do on land, so this problem is probably greater in fish farming in the sea. Salmon farms have in the past been affected by diseases that spread quickly over a wide area. In Chile the production of farmed salmon fell from 400,000 tonnes in 2008 to 130,000 tonnes in 2010 due to infectious salmon anaemia, but it had recovered by 2013 (see Asche, Cojocaru & Sikveland 2018). In 2003 the same disease broke out in the

Faeroe Islands, and production fell from 47,000 tonnes in 2004 to 12,000 tonnes in 2006 before it started to rebound.[4] The latter episode led to stricter veterinary and environmental regulations in the islands. Pandemic diseases also occur in domesticated land animals. Many readers will remember the pyres of burning animal carcasses in the English countryside after the foot and mouth disease in the early years of this century.

Salmon farming

Farmed salmon is one of the better-known farmed fish products, even if it is by no means the most important one: it accounted for only 2 per cent of the total by weight in 2018, but 7 per cent by value. Salmon farming developed from small beginnings in the 1960s. Norway was one of the pioneers, but not the only one; in 1970 250 tonnes of farmed salmon were produced in the United States, 244 tonnes in the United Kingdom and 50 tonnes in Norway. Salmon farming has languished in the United States, however, because of an unfavourable regulatory environment; in 2018 only 16,000 tonnes were produced in the country.

In Norway the regulatory environment has been more favourable, though not always uniquely benign. Figure 3.4 shows annual production of farmed salmon in Norway since 1980. The production grew almost exponentially until 2012. After that it has stagnated and rarely exceeded 1.3 million tonnes. The number for 1991 is missing, owing to a crisis in the industry, which we shall return to further on.[5] The stagnation after 2012 has been caused by a problem with parasites known as salmon lice[6] preying on the salmon, to which we shall also return; the amount produced is constrained by the number of farming licences and the amount of biomass allowed for each licence. Very few new licences have been issued since 2012, on account of the lice problem just mentioned.

The development of any industry is driven by profitability. Figure 3.5 tells an interesting story about the salmon-farming industry in Norway. It shows the price and cost per kilogram of farmed salmon from 1986 to 2018, in 2018 prices. The expansion before 1990 was driven by profitability, which in the diagram shows up as a positive difference between the price and the cost of production. Unfortunately, estimated costs are not available before 1986, and that year the price was lower than the cost of production, but this author well

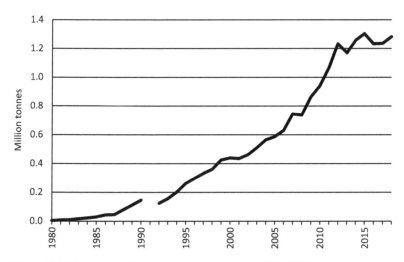

Figure 3.4 Production of farmed salmon in Norway, 1980–2018
Source: Statistics Norway.

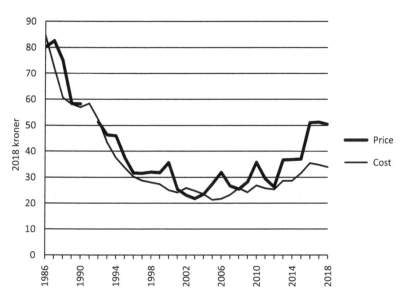

Figure 3.5 Price per kilogram (value of production divided by quantity) and cost per kilogram of farmed salmon in Norway, 2018 prices, 1986–2018
Source: Statistics Norway (quantity/value) and Directorate of Fisheries (cost).

47

remembers the expansion of the industry in the 1970s and early 1980s and the reputation it had for profitability.

Another story that emerges from Figure 3.5 is how the price and the cost of production both fell in tandem until early this century. The reason salmon farming began in the first place is that salmon was an expensive product served in white-tablecloth restaurants and on festive occasions in private homes. The price was correspondingly high: almost 170 kroner (kr) (about US$17) per kilogram to the farmer in 1980 in 2018 prices, and, needless to say, higher still in shops and restaurants. This paid for the initially high production costs. Furthemore, salmon are relatively easy to farm from the egg to the oven-ready product. Farming expanded, and the price had to yield to the increased supply, but costs also fell, as a result of technological and organizational changes. Many different factors were behind these changes: learning by doing; better construction of fish pens; changes in feeding from shovelling raw fish into the pens to feeding with pellets dispatched by automated equipment; economies of scale; selective breeding for faster-growing fish; and, undoubtedly, many other factors.

In 1990 the industry faced a crisis – temporarily, as it turned out. The price of salmon had fallen from 170 kr in 1980 to 60 kr in 1990 (in 2018 prices) and caught up with the cost of production. The organization that at the time was responsible for first-hand sales of the fish tried to control the market by taking some salmon off the market and freezing it and putting it into inventory, but it had no control over production, which continued to expand. It ended in tears: the organization went broke, but more things happened; this was not a crisis that went to waste. Before that time the salmon farming industry had been regulated in a way similar to the traditional fisheries. A dedicated sales organization had sole rights to buy fish first-hand and sell them on. The idea was that the fish-farming industry should be owned and operated by smallholders, and possibly as a part-time activity in rural areas – a backward-looking philosophy that has done untold damage to the capture fisheries in Norway. In the salmon-farming industry, such regulations were abandoned in the wake of the crisis of 1990/91, which led to the development of vertically integrated salmon-farming companies with operations in most areas of the globe where conditions and government regulations permit the farming of salmon.

It now appears that the decline in production costs in Norwegian salmon farming has run its course; since early this century they have edged upwards year by year, measured in constant value of money. The price has risen still more quickly, however, so the profitability of the industry is higher than ever before. The price rise is partly a result of the restrictive licensing policy of the Norwegian government. The rising costs are largely a result of health and environmental costs and other unspecified costs: from 2008 to 2018 the production costs of salmon rose at an annualized rate of 5 per cent while the said costs rose at a rate of almost 10 per cent, and amounted to more than 20 per cent of all costs in 2018.[7] Behind this lurks, among other things, the problem of salmon lice, already mentioned.

Because of the growth in the production of farmed salmon in Norway and other countries, it has eclipsed the production of wild salmon. In 1970 the production of farmed salmon was just over 500 tonnes while the production of wild salmon was almost 400,000 tonnes. Figure 3.6 shows the development of salmon production from that year to 2018. Most of the captured salmon is Pacific salmon; these captures have been stagnant since the early 1990s and have rarely exceeded 1 million tonnes. Most of the farmed salmon is of the Atlantic variety, even the salmon that is farmed in Chile; in 2018 over 80 per cent of all farmed salmon in Chile was Atlantic salmon. Two Pacific varieties,

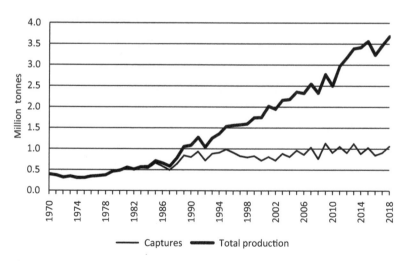

Figure 3.6 World salmon production, 1970–2018
Source: Fishery Statistical Collection (FAO).

chinook and coho, are farmed in significant quantities. Captures of Atlantic salmon are insignificant: about 2,200 tonnes in 2018. As a result of aquaculture, Atlantic salmon has grown from a white tablecloth rarity in the 1960s and 1970s to a cheap staple food today.

Norway is by far the dominant producing country for farmed salmon, accounting for almost 50 per cent of world production in 2018. Figure 3.7 shows the world production of farmed salmon 1990–2018. Chile ranked as number two in 2018, with 30 per cent of world production, followed by Scotland (6 per cent), Canada (5 per cent), the Faeroe Islands (3 per cent) and Australia (2 per cent), and then there are a number of countries producing the remaining 3 per cent. The outbreak of salmon disease in Chile around 2010 is very visible in the figure. Only a limited number of locations the world over are suitable for farming salmon in the sea. The ocean temperature must vary within a certain range; Mowi's *Salmon Farming Industry*

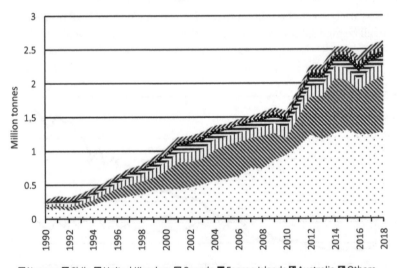

□ Norway ⬛ Chile ⊞ United Kingdom ⊟ Canada ⬛ Faeroe Islands ⊡ Australia ▨ Others

Figure 3.7 Top six producers of farmed salmon in the world, 2018
Source: Fishery Statistical Collection (FAO).

Handbook shows a band of ideal temperatures in the range from 8 to 14°C and mentions temperatures of 4 to 18°C as limits within which salmon thrive well (Mowi 2019: 50). Two further conditions are important: (a) the waters where the fish pens are placed should be sheltered from the rough waves of the open sea, against which the Norwegian archipelago is an ideal barrier; (b) there should be a strong enough current to remove feed and other spills so that it does not accumulate on the bottom below the fish pens. The Chilean coastline is another very suitable location, which has propelled Chile to the second place in the league of salmon farming. The Scottish archipelago and the Faeroe Islands are further advantageous locations in the Northern Hemisphere, and recently Iceland has emerged on the scene despite the absence of an archipelago and rather cool waters, comparable to the northernmost parts of Norway. Both coasts of northern North America are also suitable, but only Canada has taken advantage of that on any significant scale. In the United States, environmental and other special interests have proven a formidable obstacle, and the Alaskans do not want any competition with their wild salmon. There is some salmon farming in Japan and South Korea, and in New Zealand and Tasmania. Fully enclosed land-based fish farms are still largely on the drawing board, but if this design turns out to be economically viable it could upend the present location and structure of the industry: the main markets for salmon are located far from the farming areas, so it would make sense to place land-based salmon farms elsewhere and closer to the main markets. At the time of writing (mid-2020), two land-based salmon farms are under construction in the United States, one in Florida and another in Maryland.

The salmon-farming industry is dominated by a few large companies with worldwide operations. Figure 3.8 shows the market shares of the largest companies in four major salmon-farming territories: Norway, Chile, Scotland and North America, which largely means Canada. The top ten companies have a similar share of the industry in Norway (69 per cent) and Chile (75 per cent).[8] The industry in Scotland and North America is even more concentrated; in Scotland five companies are responsible for over 90 per cent of the production, and in North America just four. We find the Norwegian company Mowi represented among the top players in all four countries, and Grieg Seafood, another Norwegian company, is among the top players in Norway, Scotland and North America. The Japanese Mitsubishi Cermaq is among the top players in Norway, North America and Chile. Scottish Seafarms, one of the top players in Scotland, is 50 per cent owned by a Norwegian company (Lerøy Seafood), which is also engaged in

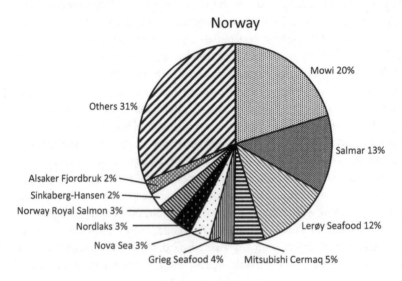

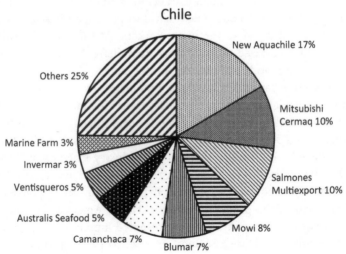

Figure 3.8 continued on next page

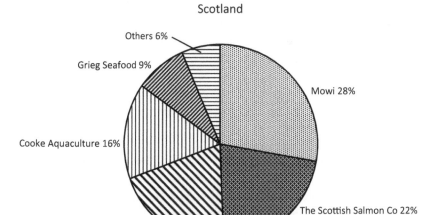

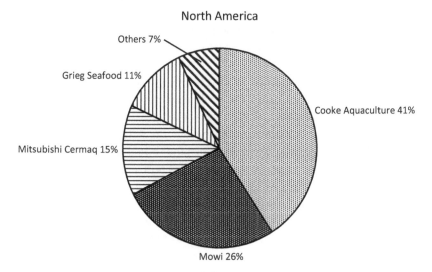

Figure 3.8 Market concentration for farmed salmon in Norway, Chile, Scotland and North America
Source: Mowi (2019).

farming sea bream and sea bass in Spain and Portugal besides capture fisheries and salmon farming in Norway. A cautionary note: the salmon-farming industry is characterized by considerable activity in terms of mergers and acquisitions and, as a consequence, name changes by companies, so this list might quickly get out of date.

Risks in salmon farming

Like other fish-farming industries, as well as animal husbandry, salmon farming faces several types of risk originating in nature. One is ripping of the fish pens. These pens are made of nets with small enough meshes so that the fish cannot ordinarily escape. Foul weather and other accidents may cause these nets to rip so that the fish can escape. For the fish farmer, this means loss of valuable capital tied up in fish that have been bought and fed towards becoming a marketable product. But it has other effects as well. Salmon that have escaped can migrate into rivers close by and interbreed with the local stock, which some experts believe has an adverse effect on the wild salmon belonging to a particular river. Salmon that return from the sea usually go back to the river where they were spawned, governed by a homing instinct that is not well understood.

Another environmental problem is the breeding of salmon lice in fish pens. Such parasites, needless to say, have a field day in that kind of environment, where the density of fish is high. Not only is it a problem for the salmon in the pen itself, but the lice spread easily through the water to wild salmon on their way back to their "home" river, and can thus be a threat for wild salmon stocks that are already critically small. This lice problem is the main reason for the halt in the expansion of the Norwegian industry, and also for the rising costs of salmon farming in Norway, as already mentioned.

Outbreaks of diseases have already been mentioned. They constitute a major risk for the industry. The consequences of infectious salmon anaemia in Chile and the Faeroe Islands were devastating, and dealing with them required shutting down production at a number of sites for months or years, which caused a substantial fall in production. Norwegian salmon farming in the 1980s was plagued by other diseases, originally fought with antibiotics, and for a time the use of such medicines reached worrying proportions. In the early 1990s salmon farmers began to use vaccines against these diseases, and the use of antibiotics fell drastically; in 1987 the use of antibiotics amounted to almost 50 tonnes, but it has rarely exceeded 1 tonne per year since 1994 despite a 27-fold increase in production from 1987 to 2018 (Mowi 2019: 92).

Yet another risk affecting salmon farmers is harmful algae blooms. These can happen in the spring and summer, when conditions for algae are particularly advantageous. The algae exhaust the oxygen available in the marine environment, suffocating the fish, and some algae also produce toxins harmful to fish. One way of avoiding these consequences is to remove the fish pens from locations with high algae concentrations to other locations, which is a costly procedure and one that requires monitoring the development of algae in a timely manner.

Price risk is yet another type of risk that fish farmers face. Compared with some other commodities, crude oil in particular, the price risk for salmon is moderate. Figure 3.9 shows the development of the price of salmon from January 2006 to June 2020. The price has increased by about 50 per cent from 2006 to 2020, not uniformly but in a wave-like fashion, reaching a high

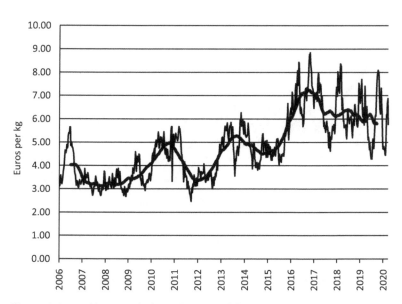

Figure 3.9 Weekly price of salmon (euros per kilogram), January 2006–June 2020
Note: smoothed curve shows annual (53 weeks) moving average.
Source: Fish Pool Index, Bergen (https://fishpool.eu).

point of €9 per kilogram before falling to about €6 in 2020. The "long waves" shown in Figure 3.9 have nothing to do with seasonality, but such might be expected for a nature-based product such as farmed salmon. Indeed, there appears to be some seasonality in the price of salmon. Figure 3.10 shows the price during the course of each year in the period from 2015 to 2019. Salmon appears to be relatively expensive from week 10 to week 30 (March through July) and cheap from week 31 to 45 (August through mid-November). From then on to the end of the year the price ticks upwards, possibly because of the holiday season. The curve for 2015 is exceptional; the price was fairly constant throughout the year until mid-November, when it rose sharply towards the end of the year.

There are now financial instruments, so-called futures contracts, that can be used to hedge against price risk in fish farming. Norwegian salmon growers can use the services of the Fish Pool exchange to fix the price of their salmon up to five years ahead. Even if price volatility is rather moderate for salmon, the salmon growers might still want to hedge against it and make sure that they can sell their final product at a price that is known when they put a brood of smolt into their pens. Suppose, for example, that

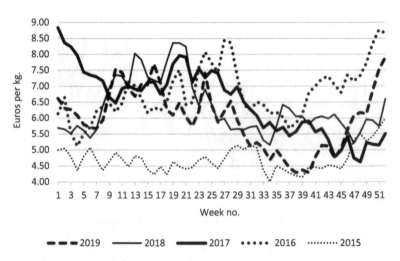

Figure 3.10 Weekly prices of salmon, 2015–19
Source: Fish Pool Index, Bergen (https://fishpool.eu).

a salmon grower put out his smolt in April 2017 and planned to sell the fish in September 2019. The futures contract for salmon to be delivered in September 2019 cost 56.25 kr per kg on 20 April 2017.[9] Suppose the grower sold a contract like that when he put out his smolt. The futures contracts are settled financially; no fish are delivered according to the contract, and the contracts are settled according to the Fish Pool price index at the time of settlement.[10] If the price index at the time of settlement is higher than the price at the time of issuing the contract the seller pays the difference to the buyer, and vice versa. Suppose the contract was settled on 2 September 2019. The Fish Pool index at that time was 47.06, so the buyer of the contract, which probably was some financial speculator, had to pay the seller, the salmon grower, 56.25 − 47.06 = 9.19 kr per kg of salmon. At about the same time the grower sold his real salmon at a price close to the Fish Pool index, as the index is an average of the price of salmon of different sizes, each size having its own, specific price. So, in reality, the salmon grower obtained a price close to the futures price of salmon at the time he sold his futures contract; he got only about 47.06 kr for his fish but made 9.19 on his futures contract, in practice selling his fish for about 56.25, the price at the time of selling the futures contract, the fall in the price of salmon being compensated for by the gain on the financial dealings.

With this trade in futures contracts, the salmon grower managed to lock in a price considerably higher than the actual price at the time he sold his fish. Not all futures trades are like this: the price could change either way; the grower would lose money if the salmon price at the time of settlement turns out to be higher than the price at the time of selling the futures contract. But the point is price certainty: the grower wants to have a guaranteed price for the product he is going to sell rather than take a gamble on the price – a gamble that could go either way. For growers with limited economic muscles, such gambles could end in tears.

Figure 3.11 illustrates that some of the price risk for Norwegian companies comes from exchange rate movements, in addition to changes in the price itself. Much of Norway's farmed salmon is exported to the euro area, mainly Germany and France. The price of salmon in the euro countries is determined by a complicated interaction between supply and demand. On the demand side, the willingness to pay for Norwegian salmon is determined in euros, which the exchange rate translates into willingness to pay the Norwegian

Figure 3.11 Price of salmon in Norwegian kroner divided by price in euros, January 2006–June 2020

Source: Fish Pool Index, Bergen (https://fishpool.eu).

salmon growers in their local currency. As the figure shows, there is some movement in the exchange rate, which at times can be substantial. It was fairly stable from the beginning of 2006 and well into 2008, when a spike of turbulence arose. Then, from early 2009, the exchange rate fell gradually, reaching a low point in the summer of 2012. Since then it has risen, with short occasional spikes, the biggest coming in early 2020. From early 2006 to early 2020 the Norwegian currency lost more than a quarter of its value in euros, falling from €0.125 per kr (8 kroner per euro) to €0.091 per kr (11 kroner per euro).

Feeding the farmed fish

The increase in farmed fish production, both marine and salmonid, as well as shrimps and prawns, is impressive, but also somewhat paradoxical, in view of the stagnation of the capture fisheries. Where do the farmed fish get their food from? Don't they eat other fish? Has the aquaculture expansion been at the expense of direct human consumption of fish? Farmed fish used to be fed on "trash fish", fish that for some reason or other was not suitable or wanted for human consumption. Early on in the development of the fish-farming industry, fish feed produced from fishmeal and fish oil was developed. The fishmeal and fish oil industry came on the stage long before the fish-farming industry, however, and fishmeal was used in feed blends for animals, mainly for pigs and poultry, because it promotes growth in these animals. Nowadays most fishmeal and fish oil is used for fish feed; about 75 per cent of fishmeal and 73 per cent of fish oil is used for fish feed.[11] The production of fishmeal and fish oil has not been any greater in recent years (2010 to 2018) than it was in the late 1970s, however, though it was somewhat greater in between. The expansion of fish farming has been made possible by increasing use of plant ingredients (rapeseed oil, soymeal, wheat) in fish feed. Figure 3.12 shows that the change in the composition of salmon feed in Norway since 1990 has been dramatic. Fishmeal and fish oil accounted for almost 90 per cent

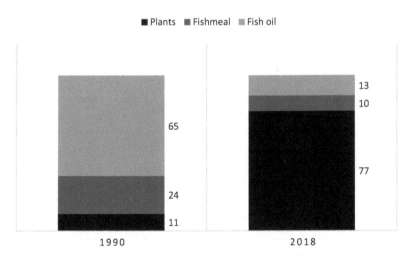

Figure 3.12 Composition (percentage) of salmon feed in Norway, 1990–2018
Source: Mowi (2019).

in 1990; by 2018 they were down to 23 per cent. The Norwegian fish feed producer Skretting maintains that it is able to produce fish feed without any input of fishmeal at all. Fish oil is more critical; currently it is not possible to produce fish feed without some minimum input of fish oil together with oil from plants.[12] One may indeed ask to what extent farmed fish are an aquatic product; they are increasingly being grown with feed from the land and just happen to be placed in holding pens in an aquatic environment. This is not necessarily a bad idea: fish have the advantage over terrestrial animals of being more efficient feed converters; fish are cold-blooded and do not need energy to keep themselves warm.

Some people are concerned about the practice of using fishmeal for fish production, arguing that this is waste of food that otherwise could sustain humans. If so, that argument would apply also to the fishmeal used in pig and poultry farming. Not all fish are amenable for human consumption, however, partly because of their taste but, more importantly, because fish flesh deteriorates quickly in high temperatures; to preserve fish for hours or more they must be chilled to near-zero temperatures, which can be a challenge in a warm climate. Some pelagic fish such as anchovy are caught in warm waters, are bony and fatty and not particularly appealing to humans even if properly preserved, which is made more difficult by their fattiness. Preserving them sufficiently well for meal production is less demanding.

A related argument is that these fish would feed other fish caught for direct human consumption if left in the water. But seabirds are probably the main competitors to humans for both anchovies and some other small pelagic fish (sardines) converted into fishmeal. When the fishmeal industry was first established in Peru it was opposed by the guano industry, which knew perfectly well where its raw material came from. The guano industry did not get a hearing, and it was dying anyway. In our days a similar issue has arisen, as some people argue that catches of anchovy and sardines and other pelagic fish should be curtailed for the benefit of seabirds and marine mammals.[13] The relevance of this argument has been challenged by Hilborn et al. (2017), who argue that seabirds and mammals typically eat younger fish that are too small to be taken by the fishing industry, which thus would not be in a direct competition with seabirds and mammals.

Yet another argument against fish farming is that having fish pass through feed processing and the digestive systems of fish or poultry is an ineffective use of a food source. Fishmeal and fish oil are 20 to 30 per cent of the raw fish measured in wet condition, which means that it takes 3.3 to 5.0 kg of feed fish to produce 1 kg of dry fish feed. It takes a bit more than a kilogram of dry feed to produce a kilogram of salmon (wet weight); one source cites 1.3 kg of dry feed being needed to produce 1.0 kg of salmon (Ellingsen & Aanondsen 2006: tab. 2). Using this number, we can conclude that it takes 4.0 to 6.5 kg of wet weight feed fish to produce 1.0 kg of salmon, given that the salmon feed is derived from feed fish only. From this we may conclude that we lose 75 to 85 per cent of the biomass of feed fish by having it transferred into salmon through fish farming. This argument is relevant, however, only if the feed fish would or could be used for direct human consumption in the first place. Market prices will signal whether it makes sense to use fish for feed or for food. Suppose farmed fish are raised exclusively by fish-based feed. If 1.0 kg of feed fish produces only 200 grams of food fish, the price of the feed fish would have to be only a fifth, or less, of the price of the food fish to make this transformation worthwhile, and less still if we account for the cost of processing the feed fish and costs other than feed costs in fish farming. In recent decades we have seen some fish species "graduate" from being mainly used for meal and oil production to food for humans. Examples are herring and mackerel, which used to be converted to fishmeal and fish oil, except for a small quantity used for human consumption, sometimes turned into delicacies by a suitable curing. This has happened because consumer markets for these species have emerged, paying prices that meal producers could not possibly compete with. The share of fish catches going wholly into meal production is declining; in recent years 25 to 35 per cent of all fishmeal and fish oil was produced from fish offal without any alternative use (FAO 2020: 8).

As an illustration, consider the unit value of two fish species landed in Norway, mackerel and blue whiting. In 2019 the value of landings divided by quantity was 15.77 kr for mackerel while for blue whiting it was 2.51 kr, so fresh landed mackerel costs more than six times as much as blue whiting. Most of the mackerel goes to direct human consumption after some processing, while the catches of blue whiting are sold to the fishmeal industry. The price of farmed salmon in 2019 was 50 kr per kg, 20 times that of blue whiting, but only about three times that of mackerel. Whether or not fish are used for direct human consumption or as an input for the fishmeal and fish oil industry is a question we can safely leave to markets to decide.

Notes

1. A shrimp and a prawn are two different animals, but similar, and especially so in taste and texture. Either of these words is often used to refer to both.
2. Not all cultivated species are fed. Carp are often left to subsist on whatever they get from their environment in earthen ponds, and, similarly, molluscs in the sea (see FAO 2018: 21). The share of unfed species of the total was 30 per cent in 2018 and has been falling over time (FAO 2020: 6).
3. The rules that apply to salmon farming in Norway, Scotland, Chile, the Faeroe Islands and Canada are discussed in Mowi's *Salmon Farming Industry Handbook* (Mowi 2019).
4. See Asche *et al.* (2010), who also mention other outbreaks of salmon diseases.
5. Statistics Norway considers the number for 1991 too unreliable to merit publication, but one can find estimates of production that year in other sources, such as the FAO Fishery Statistical Collection.
6. This is a copepod with the Latin name *Lepeophtheirus salmonis*. They attach themselves to the skin, gills and fins of the host.
7. Calculated from the profitability investigations conducted by the Directorate of Fisheries.
8. These and other percentages in this paragraph are based on a table reported in Mowi (2019: 44). The source does not say to which year this table refers.
9. Prices in this example have been taken from information available through the Fish Pool website (http://fishpool.eu).
10. For the calculation of this index, see the website of Fish Pool.
11. Numbers refer to 2018 and come from the Marine Ingredients Organisation (formerly International Fishmeal and Fish Oil Organisation, and still using the abbreviation IFFO).
12. On the possibilities of using plant-based fish feed, see Naylor *et al.* (2009).
13. See *Little Fish, Big Impact*, a report from the Lenfest Forage Fish Task Force of the Lenfest Ocean Program (2012).

4

ELEMENTARY FISHERIES ECONOMICS

The FAO database for captures of marine species contains no fewer than 1,700 species (FAO 2020: 10). The Peruvian anchovy is the top one in terms of quantity; the captures were more than 7 million tonnes in 2018, even if this was just an average year for the anchovy (see Figure 2.6). Second comes the Alaska pollock, with catches of almost 4 million tonnes in 2018 (see Figure 2.2). At the other end there are many species with catches of less than a tonne. Most fish species consist of "stocks", populations that are separated in space and with little or no interaction between them. This is the basic unit of analysis in fisheries science. Atlantic cod, for example, consists of several stocks with little or no interaction: Northeast Arctic cod, Baltic cod, Icelandic cod, North Sea cod, Northern cod of Newfoundland, and more. Some fisheries scientists think there may be subpopulations of these that could be identified as stocks in their own right.

An economic analysis of fisheries must start with some basic facts about the productivity of nature. The most basic premises are that no fish produce no fish and that fish populations would not grow without limit if left untouched by humans. Furthermore, we know that some fish stocks have been exploited for thousands of years and yet not become extinct. It makes sense, therefore, to assume that a surplus growth will be generated if stocks are reduced below the upper limit set by nature. This surplus growth can sustain fishing for ever without endangering the continued existence of the fish population; the fishery would take only whatever the population does not need to maintain itself.

Several factors may lie behind the phenomenon of surplus growth. Fishing changes the age composition of fish stocks towards younger, faster-growing cohorts. Fewer fish could mean less competition for a limited food supply (this phenomenon is likely to be stronger in confined lakes than in the open-ended ecosystems of the ocean). Older fish often eat younger individuals of the same species, so the survival of young cohorts could improve as older cohorts are depleted through fishing.

Figure 4.1 shows the surplus growth curve of a fish stock. It begins at the origin: no fish produce no fish. It intersects the horizontal axis at some point; if the stock increases beyond that point growth would become negative, and the stock would decline towards the point of intersection. For stock levels smaller than that the surplus growth is positive, and the stock would grow towards the point of intersection. It makes sense, therefore, to refer to this point of intersection as "natural equilibrium": a level a stock would tend towards if left unfished. That said, we should not expect fish stocks to remain unchanged over time if left unfished; the forces affecting growth of fish vary over time, as will be discussed in the next chapter, but for discussing some important basic principles this will do.

The mathematical formula used for generating the curve in Figure 4.1 is the well-known logistic growth function

$$G = aS\left(1 - S / K\right) \tag{4.1}$$

where G is surplus growth, a is a parameter usually called the intrinsic growth rate, S is the level of the stock and K is the carrying capacity of the environment. The parameter K is what we have called the natural equilibrium; if $S < K$ the surplus growth is positive, and vice versa, so the stock would grow or decline towards K if left alone (how the stock could possibly get beyond K is a good question and would require forces left unstated so far). This growth function is very popular in the literature on fisheries economics, but has little empirical basis other than being a simple way to produce a curve that rises from zero and then declines to intersect the horizontal axis – a relationship that agrees with the very basic stylized facts we have discussed so far. Surplus growth functions based on more realistic age-structured models, which we will discuss later in this chapter, would most likely be asymmetric, some with a maximum closer to the vertical axis than to the point of natural equilibrium (see Figure 4.10) (see Tahvonen 2009).

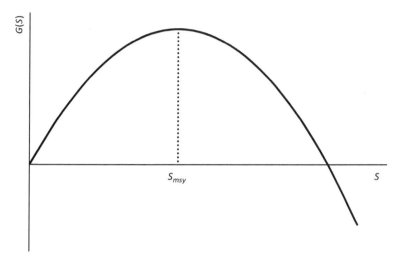

Figure 4.1 Surplus growth (G) curve of a fish stock (S)

Note: S_{msy} is the stock producing the maximum sustainable yield.

The surplus growth function sets the limits for sustainable fishing. As already stated, fishing can go on indefinitely if it takes only the surplus growth – that is, the growth in excess of what the stock needs to maintain itself. But sustainability alone does not get us very far; we see from Figure 4.1 that there are many sustainable yield levels; anything between the top of the curve and the horizontal axis is sustainable. Any given sustainable yield except the maximum has two different stock levels associated with it, a small one and a large one; the stock level producing the maximum surplus growth and sustainable yield is shown in Figure 4.1 and labelled S_{msy}. One might think that it would be better to take a given sustainable yield from the larger of the two stock levels associated with it, because (a) there would be less risk for the fish population going extinct and (b) it would be cheaper. Both these arguments take us into the world of fishing activity and how it interplays with the stock level and growth. We are about to turn to this, but, before we do so, let us consider a case when taking a sustainable yield from the smaller of the two associated stock levels might make sense. Suppose we take the maximum sustainable yield from the single stock level associated with it. Would it make economic sense to take a smaller sustainable yield from a smaller stock? We could immediately take a larger catch of fish, because we would reduce the fish stock to a lower level, but it would bring us a loss of sustainable yield in perpetuity. Could this make sense? Yes, it could, because losses sustained over infinite time have a finite value if we discount the loss in each future time period by a factor that declines over time.

A numerical example can help to clarify this. Let time be divided into distinct periods of unit length (such as years). Let the returning stock at the beginning of period t (R_t) depend on the stock left after fishing in the previous period ($S_{t-1} = R_{t-1} - Y_{t-1}$):

$$R_t = S_{t-1} + G(S_{t-1})$$

Suppose the surplus growth is given by Equation (4.1) with $a = 0.5$ and $K = 1$. The natural equilibrium stock would be equal to 1. The stock giving the maximum sustainable yield would be $S_{msy} = 0.5$, and its surplus growth would be $G(0.5) = 0.5 \times 0.5 \times 0.5 = 0.125$. Suppose we catch this quantity and keep the stock at the level 0.5, but suddenly decide to reduce the stock from 0.5 to 0.45. This would give us a gain of 0.05 by increased captures. But the smaller stock is less productive; by Equation (4.1) we calculate that $G(0.45) = 0.5 \times 0.45 \times 0.55 = 0.12375$. This would give us an annual loss for ever of $0.125 - 0.12375 = 0.00125$, compared with taking the maximum sustainable yield, from the next period onwards. How much is this worth? If we add up the losses period after period the sum would be infinite. But a loss a year from now is worth less than the same nominal loss today if we discount the future. The present value of the sum of our losses in perpetuity would be

$$\frac{0.00125}{1+r} + \frac{0.00125}{(1+r)^2} + ... = \frac{0.00125}{r}$$

where r is the discount rate.[1] With a discount rate of 5 per cent ($r = 0.05$), this would be 0.025, which is less than our once-and-for-all gain, 0.05, so it would make sense to take a smaller sustainable yield than the maximal one from a stock that is smaller than the one that produces the maximum sustainable yield.

We can derive a more general and useful expression in the following way. Our immediate economic gain from reducing the stock by a small amount ΔS would be

$$-p\Delta S$$

where p is the price of fish net of costs (and now we are saying that the cost per unit of fish caught does not depend on the size of the stock from which it is taken), ΔS is the reduction of the stock, and the minus sign comes from the fact that an increased catch of fish means a reduction of the stock level. This happens in a time interval that we can call period 0. Then comes a new period when the stock has become stabilized at a new and lower level, yielding a smaller surplus growth and sustainable yield. The value of that decline in sustainable yield is $p\Delta G$, which occurs in period 1 and all later periods. Calculating the value of this over an infinite time horizon and discounting the loss in each time period t by a factor $\dfrac{1}{\left(1+r\right)^{t}}$, where r is the discount rate, we get

$$p\Delta G\left[\frac{1}{1+r}+\frac{1}{\left(1+r\right)^{2}}+...\right]=\frac{p\Delta G}{r}$$

which is negative but finite, even if the losses occur over infinite time. Therefore, there is a trade-off between immediate gain and long-term loss. For stock levels close to the maximum of the surplus growth function the value of the long-term loss will be small, so it can be justified to move a little to the left of the maximum of the surplus growth curve until the two terms – the immediate gain and the long-term loss – become equal. Putting the immediate gain equal to the long-term loss gives

$$\Delta S=\frac{\Delta G}{r}$$

From the growth curve in Figure 4.1, we see that, for a small change in the stock (ΔS), the change in sustainable yield (ΔG) by moving slightly away from the optimal stock level (S^{o}) will be approximately equal to the slope of the tangent to the curve at that point (the derivative of the curve), which we denote as $G'(S)$, times the change in the stock, which gives

$$G'(S^o) = r \tag{4.2}$$

Since $r > 0$, the optimal stock level (S^o) is to the left of the level producing the maximum sustainable yield (Figure 4.1). The intuitive explanation is as follows. A fish left in the sea represents an investment, a deferment of benefits. If this makes sense, the fish left untaken should produce growth in the stock at a rate of $G'(S^o)$ until the next period. If the fish were caught and turned into money, that money would grow at a rate of r in the bank. Equation (4.2) thus implies the equivalence of two investment opportunities: investing in natural capital in the form of fish left in the sea and investment in financial capital by turning fish into money and putting it in the bank.

We can check that Equation (4.2) matches our numerical example by taking the derivative of Equation (4.1) with respect to S, giving

$$G'(S) = a(1 - 2S)$$

which, for $S = 0.45$, is $0.5 \times (1 - 2 \times 0.45) = 0.05$. So, if the discount rate is 5 per cent, the optimal stock would be 0.45.

The conclusion that the economically optimal stock is below S_{msy}, the stock that produces the maximum sustainable yield, is somewhat disconcerting. This is overfishing in a biological sense; the same quantity could be taken from a larger stock. In a deterministic world both situations are sustainable, but most experts would agree that smaller stocks face greater risk in a variable natural environment. We shall discuss this issue in the next chapter. One could also ask whether a stock might be so unproductive that the slope of a tangent to the growth curve is always less than the discount rate ($G'(S) < r$ for all $S > 0$). A stock such as that would be too unproductive to be fished sustainably. If the stock has a value as such regardless of its productivity it could nevertheless be worthwhile having. Finally, the result that the optimal stock level is determined by the condition $G'(S) = r$ happens only if the cost of the fish caught does not depend on the size of the exploited stock. We examine this case in the next section.

The FAO classification of fish stocks into overfished and underfished that was mentioned in Chapter 2 pertains to biological and not to economic overfishing. Biologically overfished stocks are below the S_{msy} level, while fully exploited stocks have a biomass close to S_{msy}, and underfished stocks are well above that level (see FAO 2018: 39, box 2). If the cost per unit of fish rises as a stock is depleted and discounting of the future is ignored, an economically optimal stock will always be greater than S_{msy}, and a stock could be overfished from an economic point of view even if it is not biologically overfished.

The interaction between fishing, the fish stock and stock growth

We now introduce the activities of a fishing fleet. A very popular assumption is that a unit of fishing effort always removes a certain fraction of the fish stock to which it is directed. This is built on some pretty strong assumptions about the interaction between the fish stock and the fishing fleet. First, we need some measure of the activities of the fishing fleet. For this, the notion of "fishing effort" is traditionally applied, but how it is measured varies. It could be hours of trawling, sometimes adjusted for the size of the boats involved; it could be days fishing; it could be the number of fish hooks multiplied by the time they are in the water; and much else. Note that all these definitions comprise activities directed at removing the fish from the water, which is in agreement with the original purpose: that of using change in the catch per unit of effort as a proxy for the change in the fish stock itself. But this is only a partial measure of all activities necessary to produce and bring fish to the wharf; the boats must steam to and from the fishing grounds, and they may have to spend time just to find suitable concentrations of fish. These activities also give rise to costs (time spent at sea, fuel used, etc.) and need not be directly proportional to fishing effort defined as activity directed at catching fish, but about this it is difficult to generalize. Some boats go back and forth only for the day, some spend days or months at sea until they return fully loaded. This must in principle be accounted for in economic analyses of fishing, but in this book we will adhere to the narrow definition of fishing effort as activities needed to capture fish.

If a given amount of fishing effort always captures a certain fraction of the fish stock to which it is directed, we would have the following relationship,

$$Y = qES \tag{4.3}$$

where Y is the catch of fish, E is fishing effort, S is the size of the fish stock and q is a coefficient related to the units in which we measure effort and stock, usually referred to as catchability or availability coefficient. The idealized circumstances under which this is supposed to hold are that the fish are uniformly distributed over a given area. A fishing effort of, say, an hour of trawling would sweep a certain fraction of this area and scoop up a corresponding fraction of the stock. If the fish redistribute themselves over their area as soon as the fishing gear has been removed, a repeated application of the fishing gear would again remove the same fraction of the stock, but now fewer fish, unless some new ones have been added to the population in the meantime. It is obvious that reality can be different from these idealized conditions. We shall revisit this question later in the chapter, but let us for now stick with the relationship in Equation (4.3), which, despite its shortcomings, need not be a bad approach in some real-world cases, and is in any event very popular both among fisheries economists and fisheries scientists.

Figure 4.2 connects the fishing industry with the constraints implied by surplus growth. In the left-hand panel we again have the surplus growth curve

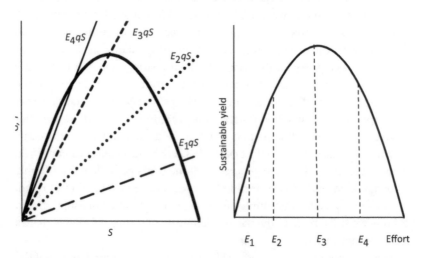

Figure 4.2 Surplus growth and production function of a fishery (left panel) and the corresponding sustainable yield curve (right panel)

and a set of lines. Each line shows the catch of fish (Y) for a given level of effort, according to Equation (4.3); the steeper the line, the greater the effort. The catch of fish rises proportionally with the stock for any given level of effort, but only the catches given by the intersection with the surplus growth curve are sustainable. If we are at a point on a line to the left and inside the surplus growth curve, the stock will grow towards the point of intersection (there is some surplus growth left over after fishing to replenish the stock); and, if we are at a point to the right and outside the curve, the stock will decline towards the point of intersection (the fishery takes too much and the stock cannot replenish itself).

Looking at the points of intersection, we see that the sustainable yield rises with fishing effort up to a certain point and then declines. The right-hand panel of Figure 4.2 shows the sustainable yield as a function of fishing effort. Mathematically, we put Equations (4.1) and (4.3) equal, which gives us the sustainable stock level (S_{sust}) as a function of effort:

$$S_{sust} = K\left(1 - Eq / a\right) \tag{4.4}$$

Inserting this stock level into Equation (4.3) gives us sustainable yield as a function of effort:

$$Y_{sust} = \alpha E - \beta E^2, \alpha = qK, \beta = q^2 K / a \tag{4.5}$$

Some fundamental economic relationships

In Figure 4.3 (upper panel), we have sustainable yield in terms of value. At a price independent of the quantity landed it looks exactly like the sustainable yield function in terms of quantity; we need only to scale the vertical axis differently. In this figure, we also see the total cost of fishing at a constant cost per unit of effort for two different values of that cost parameter. Later we shall relax these somewhat special assumptions about a given price of fish independent of the quantity caught and a constant unit cost of fishing effort, but they turn out not to have serious consequences for the results presented.

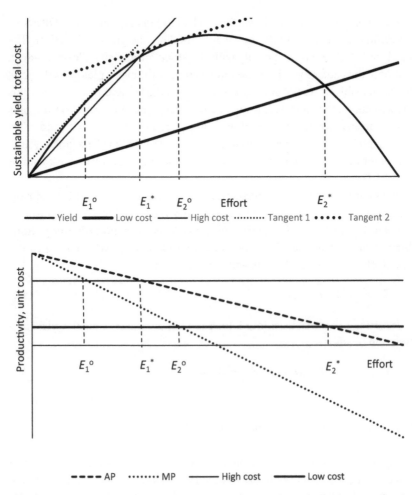

Figure 4.3 Production value at a constant price and total cost for "high" versus "low" cost per unit of effort (upper panel) and average and marginal productivity and "high" versus "low" cost per unit of effort (lower panel)

What situation are we likely to end up with in the fishery? Fish stocks are seldom privately owned,[2] and they used to be open-access resources, meaning that everyone who so desired could set out to sea and fish them. Fish stocks were at least partly and sometimes wholly accessible in waters outside national jurisdiction. In the 1970s the so-called exclusive economic zone was established, giving coastal states regulatory power over fish stocks, sometimes entirely and sometimes jointly with other states when stocks migrate between different jurisdictions. We shall consider this issue in Chapters 6 and 7, but the open-access case is still useful as a benchmark, and in some cases access is practically open for all people of the right nationality even if fish stocks have come under national jurisdiction.

In the absence of access regulations, actual and potential fishermen or fishing firms will compare the value of their potential fish catch to what it would cost to get it. They are likely to enter the fishing industry, or expand their activities, if they expect their revenues from fishing to exceed their costs. If all fishermen are equally skilled or equally well equipped, we can expect economic equilibrium (no tendency to change the total effort) when total costs are equal to total revenues. Revenues per unit of effort will then be equal to the cost per unit of effort.

In Figure 4.3 (upper panel) we see two such equilibria, E_1^* and E_2^*, each corresponding to its particular cost per unit of effort. We see that they occur on either side of the maximum sustainable yield curve. Curiously, perhaps, the low-cost case results in less sustainable yield, but more fishing effort, than the high-cost case. This indicates that all is not well with the economic situation likely to prevail in an open-access fishery. Normally, one would expect a lower cost of production to result in greater output, but in the open-access fishery the opposite can happen.

What goes wrong is clarified by the lower panel of Figure 4.3. The downward-sloping lines show average and marginal productivity, labelled *AP* and *MP*. The average productivity is simply the value of production divided by fishing effort. The marginal productivity is, mathematically speaking, the derivative of the sustainable yield function (the slope of a line tangential to the sustainable yield function) multiplied by price. In less technical language, it is the value of the contribution of the last unit of effort to the sustainable yield. This is much less than the average product-ivity. As already stated, we get an economic equilibrium in an open-access fishery when the average productivity is equal to the cost per unit of effort. In this situation, the last unit of effort is not paying for itself; it contributes less to the total value produced by the fishery than it costs.

Why is the marginal productivity less than the average productivity? Each additional unit of effort, or boat added to the fishery, will reduce the fish stock, which in turn reduces the fish catches other boats will take with any given effort. This must be subtracted from the catches of the additional boat to get the net contribution of that additional boat to the fishery. This is why that contribution could be negative, even if the boat is catching just as much fish as all other boats. The fish stock would then be overexploited in the biological as well as the economic sense. But the individual boat owners have no incentive to take into account how other boat owners are affected by their fishing effort; they are concerned only with what they get themselves. Only if the fishery were dominated by one or a few large companies, or governed by some kind of cooperative or trust, would such effects be taken into account when making decisions on how much effort or how many boats to apply.

The economically optimal level of fishing effort is given by the intersection of the marginal productivity line with the line showing the cost per unit of effort. For the two cost cases in Figure 4.3, these are the effort levels E_1° and E_2°. As we see in the lower panel of Figure 4.3, this implies less effort than would result from open access, and the optimal effort would not exceed the effort producing maximum sustainable yield. This result could be modified, however, if we discount future revenues, as we shall return to shortly; here we are comparing two equilibrium (sustainable) situations, ignoring the eventual transition to a new equilibrium, such as was discussed in the previous section.

Economically optimal effort implies that the difference between revenues and costs is maximized. This difference goes by the name of resource rent or fishing rent, as this is a revenue in excess of all necessary costs and could in principle be extracted by a presumptive owner of the fish stock. This is indicated in Figure 4.3 (upper panel) by the difference between the cost line and a parallel line (dotted) tangent to the sustainable yield curve. In mathematical terms, the optimal effort can be derived by maximizing the resource rent, but it is more doubtful whether this should be the objective of fisheries policy. For a hypothetical owner of a fish stock, or for a government planning to use the rent as a source of income, this would make sense, but it makes even better sense in terms of economic policy to maximize the overall efficiency in the economy, in which case it is necessary that each unit of effort, or boat, contributes a net value to the fishery equal to its cost. This, as already stated, implies maximization of the fishing rent, even if maximization of this rent is not the primary goal of fisheries policy.

A more general approach

How critical are the simplifying assumptions we have made so far? We have ignored a possible dependence of the price on the quantity fished. Relaxing this assumption would affect the shape of the sustainable yield function, but not the conclusion that open access results in overfishing. We could end up with more than one economic equilibrium, but all of them would imply fishing effort exceeding the optimal effort (see Anderson 1973). We have also assumed that the cost per unit of effort is constant. Relaxing this would mean that instead of a straight line we would have a cost curve rising at an increasing rate. In economic equilibrium the last unit of effort would break even; the cost of the marginal unit of effort would be equal to the catch value per unit of effort, but less expensive units (boats, fishermen) would earn a profit over and above their cost. These profits would be due to whatever causes cost differences between fishermen, whether skill, equipment or whatever.[3] But open access would still result in an effort greater than optimal; the marginal productivity would still be below the cost of the marginal unit of effort.

This picture of the fishing industry in which there is a marked difference between fishermen is more familiar to connoisseurs of the industry than the simple model of fishermen being alike in terms of costs and skills.[4] The Icelandic economist Ágúst Einarsson tells a story from the town of Vestmannaeyjar, where he grew up. A young fisherman applied for a loan to buy a new boat. The bank asked for a business plan. This was an unfamiliar exercise for the young man. Instead, he had his picture taken with a collection of trophies that the number one fisherman of the year had earned; he had done so several years in a row. He sent the picture to the bank in lieu of the business plan – and got the loan (see Einarsson 2016: 125–6).

The shape of the surplus growth curve could affect the shape of the sustainable yield curve in a non-trivial way. The surplus growth curve need not begin at the origin; there could be some critical minimum viable stock level below which the growth is negative. In a similar vein, the relative rate of surplus growth need not fall uniformly; it could be rising for small stock levels. Even so, open access would still result in excessive fishing effort. Worse, it could result in extinction of the stock, and the extinction risk would increase with the profitability of the fishery.[5]

As was said earlier, the assumption leading to Equation (4.3), on which we have built our analysis so far, is rather special: a fish stock evenly spread over a given area. What if the fish stock spreads itself over a smaller area if it declines in size? The density of the stock would no longer be proportional to its size, and our hypothetical trawler would scoop up a larger share of the stock the smaller it is. One way of taking this into account is to use a more flexible production function:

$$Y = qES^b, 0 \leq b \leq 1 \tag{4.3'}$$

The case considered so far is $b = 1$, but if $b < 1$ the density of the fish stock does not fall in proportion to its size, and in the limiting case of $b = 0$ it is constant and independent of the size of the stock. This has devastating consequences for the economic equilibrium. The catch per unit of effort would be constant and always the same irrespective of whether the stock is large or small. If the value of the catch per unit of effort exceeds the cost per unit of effort there will always be an incentive to expand effort until the stock has been wiped out. Unfortunately, this case, or something close, is not unlikely to hold for fish that aggregate and travel in large shoals. The near-extinction of the Norwegian spring-spawning herring in the late 1960s, to be discussed in the next chapter, may have been the result of this.[6] As one fisheries biologist put it, the last shoal of herring could be large enough to fill up your boat. With this more flexible function, the overexploitation of open access still holds and is aggravated by a greater risk of extinction as a result of overfishing.

It is worthwhile pointing out that the case of $b < 1$ makes the catch per unit of effort a misleading and possibly useless index for the size of a fish stock. From (Equation 4.3') we have $\frac{Y}{E} = qS^b$, and the catch per unit of effort would decline less than the stock. A weakness of this signal is believed to have been one reason why the Norwegian spring-spawning herring and the Northern cod of Newfoundland collapsed. These episodes will be discussed in the next chapter.

Lastly, what about discounting of the future? Focusing on sustainable yields implicitly ignores discounting and looks only at one period assumed to be like all others, ignoring possible transitions to a biological equilibrium with a stable stock. A more general formulation would show that discounting reduces the optimal equilibrium stock. Two economic forces pull the optimal equilibrium stock in opposite directions: discounting of the future pulls it downwards, whereas the stock-dependent unit cost of fish caught pulls it upwards (Clark 1976). If the unit cost of fish is independent of the stock, the effect of discounting prevails, and the optimal stock is always smaller than the one producing the maximum sustainable yield as long as the discount rate is positive. We have already looked at this case (Equation 4.2). If the discount rate is zero and the unit cost of fish is stock-dependent, the optimal stock will always be above the maximum sustainable yield level. With both forces acting, the result will be somewhere in between. Whether or not the unit cost of fish caught depends on the stock depends in turn on the production function. Using Equation (4.3') we get, for the unit cost of fish caught (c_y),

$$c_y = \frac{cE}{qES^b} = \frac{c}{qS^b} \qquad (4.6)$$

where c is the cost per unit of effort. If $b = 0$, the unit cost of fish is constant and independent of the stock. As mentioned above, herring and other schooling fish might be close to this case. If $b = 1$, the cost per unit of fish caught is inversely proportional to the stock size. This, or something close, is often believed to be the case for bottom-dwelling fish such as cod. In general, the closer b is to 1, the more the unit cost of fish caught depends on the stock.

Age-structured models

The fish stock model presented so far is characterized as a "biomass" model: a given tonnage of fish grows or declines according to some mathematical formula. Such models are useful for deriving important qualitative results, such as the overexploitation and inefficiency prevailing in an uncontrolled, open-access fishery. Such models have also been used in applied work at a stage when there was little information available on fish stocks. The first things people know about a fishery are how much fish has been captured and by how many boats, and even these data can be subject to incomplete and perhaps deliberately false reporting. The industry and the public authorities will have to do with whatever information they have on fish captures and the activities of the fishing fleet. In the early stages one can look at the catches per unit of fishing effort and proceed on the basis of Equation (4.3) above. Later, as a fishery develops, there will be resources and scope for more systematic data gathering, both by captures for research purposes and from samples based on commercial captures.

Fish stocks do not consist of homogeneous "biomass", however, but of individuals, each with their specific weight and age. The development of a fish stock depends on how these individuals grow and survive, as well as on new individuals entering the population. In the nineteenth century scientists discovered that growth in fish leaves a ring structure in their scales and bones, like rings in a tree trunk, making it possible to determine their age. The most common bone used for this purpose is the otolith, a bone in the fish's head. By analysing the otoliths and examining how the number of rings relates to the size (length) of individual fish, it is possible to divide a sample of fish into age classes. Doing this over time makes it possible to analyse how the age composition of captured fish changes over time. This in turn makes it possible to estimate the mortality rate in the underlying fish population. Fish captures are due to the fish mortality caused by fishing, and how fish captures evolve over time depends on how the number of fish develops over time, as well as the growth over time of the fish that survive.

From these premises, fisheries scientists construct numerical models of fish populations. This is, needless to say, not an exact science. A fisheries scientist has put it like this: "Counting fish is just like counting trees, except that you don't see them and they move." Yet these models are in many cases quite successful in predicting fish catches a few years ahead, and even more so in explaining the variability of fish catches in the past. We shall return to the point about variability in the next chapter, but focus on explaining these models in a deterministic environment in the present one.

If we start with N_0 fish of age h_0, in year t_0, over time their number will evolve according to the formula

$$N_1 = N_0 \exp\left(-s_{h_0} F_{t_0} - M_{h_0}\right), \tag{4.7}$$

$$N_2 = N_1 \exp\left(-s_{h_0+1} F_{t_0+1} - M_{h_0+1}\right) = N_0 \exp\left(-\sum_{t=t_0}^{t_0+1} \left(s_{h_0+(t-t_0)} F_t + M_{h_0+(t-t_0)}\right)\right),$$

...

$$N_T = N_0 \exp\left(-\sum_{t=t_0}^{t_0+T-1} \left(s_{h_0+(t-t_0)}F_t + M_{h_0+(t-t_0)} \right) \right)$$

The parameters F and M denote the mortality rates resulting from fishing and natural reasons (by "natural" reasons, we mean predation by other fish or disease). These are instantaneous rates, not annual rates. An advantage of using instantaneous rates is that these rates are additive; a fish cannot die simultaneously for two different reasons (fishing and natural reasons). Annual rates are not additive; a fish that is caught some time during a year might have been eaten by other fish before the year is over. An annual mortality rate of 1 means that all fish die before the year is over. This would require an instantaneous rate of infinity (put different values of x into the expression $\exp(-x)$ and see what happens).

One thing that makes Equation (4.7) complicated is that we must keep track of two time schedules. One is calendar time. Fishing mortality occurs in calendar time; in year t the fishing fleet exerts a certain amount of activity generating fishing mortality. Therefore, F is indexed by t, beginning in calendar year t_0, when N_0 of fish were available at the beginning of the year. The other time schedule is the age of the fish. They were assumed to become available at age h_0. This need not be age zero, the year they were spawned; for some slow-maturing fish species, h_0 could be several years. For Northeast Arctic cod, for example, h_0 is usually considered three years, and, even so, very few fish at that age are caught by the gear used by the fishing fleets involved. We need to keep track of the age of the fish because of the parameters s_h and M_h, and also because of the weight of the fish, to which we shall return shortly. The parameter s_h expresses how vulnerable the fish are to the fishing gear. The gear "selects" fish differently according to size. Small fish escape through the meshes of trawls, and trawl nets are in fact often deliberately made with large meshes as needed to let fish below a certain age escape, in order to save them for later capture when they have grown bigger. Mesh sizes are, in fact, one of the parameters of fisheries policy. Therefore, s is indexed by $h = h_0 + t - t_0$, where t_0 is the calendar time this particular cohort became available for the fishery at age h_0.

When fisheries scientists estimate mortality from the age compositions of catch samples, they are primarily able to estimate total mortality, $F + M$. There is very little knowledge available about what natural mortality is. It is likely to vary over time and also to vary with the age of the fish, but usually it is just assumed constant at some reasonable level; the rates of 0.15 and 0.2 are frequently used in stock assessment models. For some stocks, however, fisheries scientists believe they have enough information to let natural mortality vary with age, usually so that it is highest for the youngest age groups. We shall see an example of that below. Likewise, it is difficult to estimate the gear selectivity parameter s. One would expect it to vary from zero to 1, with fish gradually becoming fully selected, but in applications one frequently sees values of $s > 1$, where s then is referenced to some fish of "middle age" that are most vulnerable to the gear, with older and younger fish being less so. Selectivity typically varies significantly from one gear to another; it is different for gill nets, long lines and hand lines, as well as for trawls with meshes of different size.

To find the catches of fish in numbers from a cohort of fish in a particular year, also called year class, we calculate the number of fish that have died during the year, $N_t - N_{t+1}$ (Equation 4.7). The fraction $F_t/(F_t+M)$ must have been taken by the fishery. But we are usually interested in the size of fish catches in terms of weight, not numbers. We can find this by multiplying by the average weight of the fish during the year, a parameter $w(h)$ if we are looking at fish of age h. This is a bit imprecise; fish grow continuously, and, if most of them are caught early in the year, their average weight in the catch will be less than their average weight in the stock. This can be dealt with by using a growth function in continuous time and integrating the whole fish yield equation over one year, as Raymond Beverton and Sidney Holt (1957) did in their pioneering work on age-structured models. The gain in precision is likely to be small, however. One reason is that fish growth can in fact vary over the year, and the catching activity is typically somewhat or even markedly seasonal, occurring over only a part of the year.

If we analyse an equilibrium situation in which the fishing mortality is always the same, the fish yield function is comparatively simple. All we need to do is to follow a cohort of fish over its life history, because the number of fish of any given age will always be the same at all times. This gives the following expression, which is easily put into a spreadsheet:

$$Y = \sum_{h=h_0}^{\max h} \frac{s_h F}{s_h F + M_h} N_{h_0} \exp\left(-\sum_{i=h_0}^{h-1} (s_i F + M_i) \right) w(h) \left[1 - \exp(-s_h F - M_h) \right]$$

$$(4.8)$$

The first exponential term tracks the development of the cohort since it first appeared. For $h = h_0$, the sum does not exist and we have $\exp(0) = 1$. The next year, $h = h_0 + 1$, the population has been reduced by a factor $\exp\left(-s_{h_0} F - M_{h_0}\right)$, and so on. The cut-off point max h is arbitrary; fish can live for quite a long time, but at some age there are so few of them left that we can ignore older age groups.

An equilibrium model such as this is useless for predictions or backward-looking analyses of fish populations, because of natural fluctuations (to be discussed in the next chapter) and also because fishing mortality (F) varies from year to year. But it is useful for analysing the effects of changing the selectivity of fishing gear, or finding out what the most appropriate fishing mortality would be. Indeed, as we shall see, the optimal fishing mortality depends on the gear selectivity profile, and, if the latter can be changed, the two should be optimized simultaneously. It is straightforward to amend this model to forecast the fish yield for a specified number of years into the future, however, or to ascertain whether it explains past catches reasonably well. Suppose we start in year 0 with an estimated number of fish of ages h_0 to max h. For a fishing mortality of F_0 in year 0, the yield of fish in year 0 would be

$$Y_0 = \sum_{h=h_0}^{\max h} \frac{s_h F_0}{s_h F_0 + M_h} N_{h,0} w(h)\left[1 - \exp\left(-s_h F_0 - M_h\right)\right] \tag{4.8'}$$

Then, for the next year, one would update the number of fish of age $h > h_0$ by

$$N_{h+1,1} = N_{h,0} \exp\left(-s_h F_0 - M_h\right), h = h_0, \ldots, \max h - 1$$

What about $N_{h_0,1}$, the youngest cohort the next year? This, usually called "recruitment", depends on the survival of the eggs spawned a certain number of years before. For years in the past, we may have estimates of recruitment. For the future, one could use a recruitment function to determine this, but such functions are notoriously difficult to estimate and the apparently random variability in recruitment is enormous. These issues will be discussed later in this chapter. Average recruitment is often employed, to get a rough idea about fish catches for the next few years. Updating for subsequent years follows the same logic.

An example: the Northeast Arctic cod

The Northeast Arctic cod has been exploited for over a thousand years. The Sagas tell us that this fishery was a source of income for the Norwegian kings in the ninth century. This fish stock is also one of the most researched ones in the world. It is managed jointly by Norway and Russia, as it migrates between the waters of these two countries, but some third countries are also permitted to catch some fish from this stock. Here we shall use data about this stock to illustrate the age-structured model just discussed (ICES 2019a).[7] The model we look at is given by Equation (4.8), with a constant recruitment – that is, the number of fish coming into the stock every year. We fix this number at 770 million individuals, the average number of three-year-old fish entering the stock from 1946 to 2018. It may appear unrealistic to assume a constant recruitment of fish; one would think that it would depend on the size of the mature stock spawning the roe and the milt. We shall revisit this question below. Yet, for a wide size range of the spawning stock, the size of year classes recruited to the fishery appears fairly independent of the spawning stock size, so our conclusions are little affected by this assumption, except for extreme sizes of the spawning stock. Models such as this go by the name of yield per recruit models, as it is essentially the catch per fish recruited we are looking at.

Table 4.1 shows the parameters used in the model of the Northeast Arctic cod. We consider 19 age groups of ages 3–21. Fish come into the stock as three-year-olds, and even at that age they are seldom caught (the selectivity parameter is only 0.0184, which can be interpreted as the risk for fish of getting caught if they encounter the fishing gear). The cut-off age of 21 is arbitrary, but very few fish are left at that age. The selectivity pattern of the fishery is a bit strange (Figure 4.4).[8] It rises almost linearly up to a full selection of 11-year-old fish, and then falls to quite low levels for fish 14 years of age and older. This is most likely caused by a multitude of fishing gears, each with its own selectivity being applied in specific areas. Figure 4.5 shows the age-specific weight of fish and the curve fitted to these observations and used in the model.[9] The parameters for maturity define the spawning stock.

Table 4.1 Parameters for Northeast Arctic cod

Age	Selectivity	Weight	Maturity	M
3	0.0184	0.127	0	0.3479
4	0.1135	0.452	0.003	0.2445
5	0.2919	1.039	0.033	0.2382
6	0.4740	1.906	0.199	0.2201
7	0.6313	3.049	0.624	0.2
8	0.7673	4.448	0.894	0.2
9	0.7970	6.074	0.947	0.2
10	0.8938	7.895	0.988	0.2
11	1.0000	9.874	0.997	0.2
12	0.7039	11.978	1	0.2
13	0.4218	14.174	1	0.2
14	0.2802	16.431	1	0.2
15	0.2802	18.722	1	0.2
16	0.2802	21.024	1	0.2
17	0.2802	23.315	1	0.2
18	0.2802	25.579	1	0.2
19	0.2802	27.800	1	0.2
20	0.2802	29.967	1	0.2
21	0.2802	32.070	1	0.2

Source: ICES (2019a).

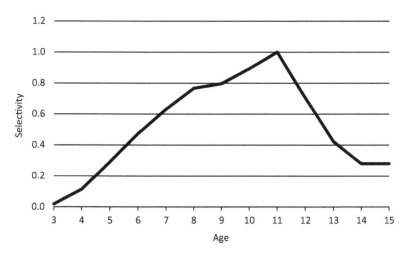

Figure 4.4 Selectivity pattern in the fishery for Northeast Arctic cod

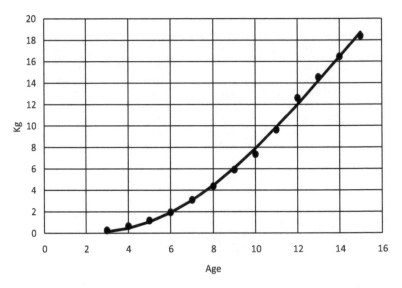

Figure 4.5 Average weight of fish aged 3–15 years (points) and a von Bertalanffy growth curve fitted to these observations

Figure 4.6 shows the sustainable catch of fish for different selectivity patterns and different values of fishing mortality. Note that the curve flattens out to the right. This happens because we have assumed that a certain number of fish will always replenish the stock every year, no matter how intensely it is exploited. This means that the curve approaches the total biomass of the cohort of recruits (three-year-old fish) asymptotically as fishing mortality increases; as it approaches infinity it would scoop up all the young fish immediately. These fish are sexually immature, so no spawning stock would exist to produce new recruits, so this is patently unrealistic. We address that question below, but suffice it at this point to say that most of the relevant action is in the left part of the diagram, which is not much affected by this unrealistic assumption.

The lowest of the yield curves comes from the actual selectivity pattern in the fishery (selectivity 1). It rises to a maximum of 756,000 tonnes for a fishing mortality of $F = 0.35$. For comparison, the average catch of Northeast Arctic

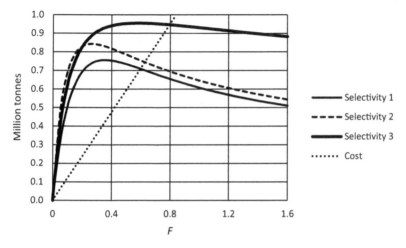

Figure 4.6 Sustainable catch of fish as a function of fishing mortality (F) and gear selectivity

Note: "Selectivity 1" is the pattern observed in ICES (2019a); the dotted line shows cost rising linearly with fishing mortality.

cod from 1946 to 2018 was 672,000 tonnes, with a maximum and a minimum of 1,343,000 and 212,000 tonnes respectively. As fishing mortality increases beyond $F = 1.0$ the sustainable yield falls below 600,000 tonnes, but we are then getting into a situation in which the spawning stock is becoming quite small, and conclusions based on constant recruitment are becoming risky.

As already noted, the selectivity pattern is curious, as "old" fish seem to be much less vulnerable to the fishing gear than fish of "middle age". What, then, if all fish 11 years and older were fully selected ($s_h = 1$ for $h \geq 11$)? We let the selectivity parameter rise linearly from $s_3 = 0$ to $s_{11} = 1$ and keep it at $s = 1$ for older age groups. This produces the second yield curve (selectivity 2) in Figure 4.6. We see that it produces more fish for all values of fishing mortality and has a maximum of $F = 0.3$ with a catch of 840,000 tonnes, considerably more than the present pattern of selectivity.

Why does this happen? Figure 4.7 provides an explanation. It shows the weight at age of individual fish, and that weight is still increasing almost

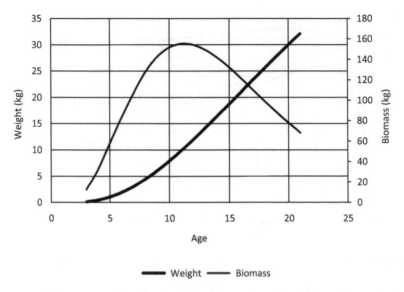

Figure 4.7 Weight at age for individual fish (left axis) and total weight (biomass) of a cohort of 100 fish at the age of three, subject to natural mortality as shown in Table 4.1 (right axis)

linearly at the age of 20. But, if left unfished, fish of a given cohort are dying at a rate of 0.2 or more (see Table 4.1). The figure shows the total weight of the surviving fish from an initial cohort of 100. We see that it reaches its maximum at the age of 11. Leaving older fish in the sea means a loss of biomass, and catches could be increased by catching them at a higher rate.

If we could select perfectly the age at which to take the fish, we would catch them as 11-year-olds. Such perfect selection is not possible, but we might be able to change our fishing gear or fishing methods so that we take more of them at a younger age than now. With selectivity pattern 3 the selectivity changes linearly from zero at the age of 6 to 1 at the age of 16. This produces the third and highest yield curve in Figure 4.6, with a maximum of 955,000 tonnes for $F = 0.6$. Why this? Fish at 6 years old are a lot younger than they are at 11 years old. But we cannot wait to catch them all at the age of 11, and the chosen selectivity pattern is symmetric around 11, the age of maximum unexploited biomass.

It was noted that selectivity and fishing mortality should be optimized simultaneously; changing one and ignoring the other may not accomplish a great deal. Before management by fish quotas (to be discussed in Chapter 8), limits to the number of fishing days and other modern management measures came along, gear selectivity was one of the major issues in fisheries management. Fisheries managers and scientists would point out that fish yields could be increased by sparing more of the young, fast-growing fish. But, economically, such measures alone may achieve little or nothing. Suppose that fishing costs rise linearly with fishing mortality, as indicated by the dotted line in Figure 4.6. This would be the case if fishing mortality is proportional to fishing effort; this is the case we discussed earlier, when the fishing gear sweeps a certain fraction of the area where the fish are always evenly distributed and scoops up a certain fraction of the stock. Suppose we have an open-access fishery with selectivity profile 1 that has reached the economic equilibrium. This is where $F = 0.6$ and the sustainable yield is 714,000 tonnes. Along come fisheries scientists and point out that the yield could be increased by choosing a different selectivity pattern, such as selectivity 3. Suppose this is agreed. Over time the sustainable yield would increase to 955,000 tonnes if the fishing mortality remains unchanged, but it will not unless access to the fishery is controlled somehow. With increased catches, profits would emerge in the fishery, leading to increased effort under open access. We would get a new economic equilibrium at which the cost line crosses the new yield curve at $F = 0.8$ and the sustainable yield is 946,000 tonnes. Catches have indeed increased, but the fishery is just as inefficient as it used to be; the marginal fishing boat is not paying for itself, and the same catch could be taken with about one-half of the effort.

Let us finally consider the question of what might happen to the recruitment of fish as fishing mortality is increased. This is bound to reduce the spawning stock, which in turn would ultimately affect recruitment. But, strange as it may seem, it has proved very difficult to find a significant relationship between the size of the spawning stock and the recruitment it produces. This is true for all stocks known to this author. What we see is a lot of variability, from which it is nearly impossible to identify a relationship between the spawning stock and the number of recruits. There is little doubt that a larger spawning stock produces more roe and milt, but there are simply too many things happening to these small creatures before the fish eggs are fertilized and they metamorphose into recognizable fish; most of them get eaten by other fish. Getting the appropriate food at the right time may be critical for survival, and by no means certain (see, for example, Toresen *et al.* 2019).

Figure 4.8 shows what the situation looks like for the Northeast Arctic cod. The variability of recruitment is simply enormous. In most years recruitment is mediocre, but every once in while an exceptionally good recruitment occurs, and it seems unrelated to the size of the spawning stock, except that unusually large spawning stocks have not produced large recruitment. Two recruitment curves, popular in the literature, have been fitted to these observations and are shown in the figure.[10] Both are about equally unsuccessful in explaining the variability of recruitment. These recruitment curves are specified as follows:

$$R = \frac{aS}{1 + S / K} \text{ (Beverton–Holt)} \tag{4.9}$$

$$R = aS \exp(-bS) \text{ (Ricker)} \tag{4.10}$$

where R is recruitment and S is the spawning stock, and a, K and b are the estimated parameters. We shall use both of these to complete the model of the Northeast Arctic cod. We let S be determined by Equation (4.7) through the development of the cohort $(N_0, ..., N_{max\,h})$ and the maturity parameters in Table 4.1, looking for a consistent solution where $R = N_0$. Each of these two recruitment functions produces its own unrealistic outcomes. Figure 4.9 shows the sustainable yield produced by the two functions. The yield now falls uniformly, as fishing mortality is increased beyond the maximum sustainable yield level, and hits zero when fishing mortality has become so high as to wipe out the spawning stock. This critical fishing mortality is somewhat different for the two functions.

The Beverton–Holt function gives a higher sustainable yield and the corresponding fishing mortality is much lower: 0.25 compared with 0.8 in the Ricker model. This happens because the Beverton–Holt function produces much higher recruitment for large spawning stocks such as would result from a low fishing mortality. The Ricker function produces the largest recruitment for a relatively small spawning stock (just below 1 million tonnes), and the high fishing mortality of 0.8 produces a spawning stock close to that size.

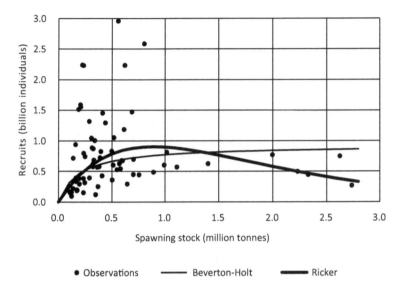

Figure 4.8 Recruitment of three-year-old fish (dots) plotted against the size of the spawning stock that produced them and two recruitment curves fitted to these data by minimizing the logarithm of errors (logarithm of ratio of observations to values of the recruitment curve)
Source: ICES (2019a: tab. 3.18).

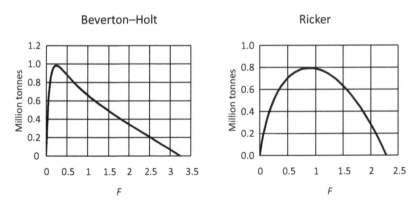

Figure 4.9 Sustainable yield of Northeast Arctic cod with a recruitment function and selectivity profile 3

A fishing mortality of 0.8 is much higher than considered appropriate for the Northeast Arctic cod (see next chapter and Figure 5.1), but the models used in assessments of this stock do not incorporate a recruitment function, except in a very crude form with a precautionary lower limit set on the spawning stock (ICES 2019a).

Figure 4.10 shows sustainable yield as a function of the total stock biomass. This is analogous to the surplus growth function shown in Figure 4.1. Both recruitment functions produce asymmetric yield functions, but they are skewed in opposite ways. The maximum sustainable yield with the Beverton–Holt function occurs with a biomass that is only one-third of the biomass in pristine equilibrium. The latter is unrealistically large, however: about 18 million tonnes. The biomass of the stock was 4.3 million tonnes in 1946, just after the Second World War, during which the stock was lightly exploited. It seems difficult to reconcile the Beverton–Holt function with what the stock would probably be in a natural equilibrium without exploitation. One possibility is cannibalism; old cod eat younger cod, and this would undoubtedly increase if the fish survive longer (see Yaragina, Bogstad & Kovalyev 2009). This would produce increased natural mortality, which would reduce the natural equilibrium stock.

The Ricker function produces a more realistic value for the natural equilibrium stock: just below 4 million tonnes. The yield curve is asymmetric in a way opposite to the Beverton–Holt case, with a maximum for a stock about two-thirds of what it would be in a natural equilibrium. As we have seen, the

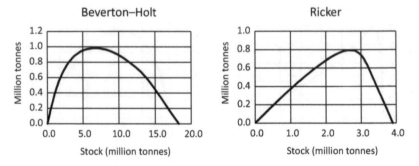

Figure 4.10 Sustainable yield plotted against the total stock biomass (selectivity profile 3)

Ricker curve produces a distinct maximum for a relatively small spawning stock, which has the effect of producing a rather high fishing mortality for maximizing sustainable yield, much higher than usually considered likely for this particular stock.[11] In their stock assessment reports, fisheries biologists seldom use a recruitment function; instead, they assume a constant recruitment, which may be reasonable for the range of fishing mortalities and stock sizes they are considering. If, however, constant recruitment is believed to be reasonable for all stock levels larger than some minimum, some other mechanism is needed to produce reasonable values for a hypothetically unexploited stock, such as rising predation mortality of juveniles and younger cohorts as older cohorts become more plentiful.

Ricker's recruitment model

This chapter concludes with a few more remarks on William Ricker's recruitment model. It was originally developed for Pacific salmon, which spawn in rivers in the United States and Canada, go to sea as immature fish and return as mature fish several years later to their home river to spawn (Ricker 1958, 1975). Pacific salmon spawn only once, so the Ricker model is a two-cohort model, with a parent cohort and an offspring cohort. Many of the fish perish during their stay in the sea, but for a given natural mortality while in the sea the size of the "runs" returning to their home rivers depends on the size of the stock leaving the river many years before. Many of the salmon are fished nearshore before they enter the rivers, and the management of the salmon fishery is to a large extent about allowing a sufficient number of fish to escape capture and get into the rivers to reproduce. Ricker developed his model for this purpose.

The model specification is slightly different from the one we used earlier; the parameter a in Equation (4.10) is equal to one, as both R and S are measured at the same age, and we use a instead of b in the exponential term:

$$R_{t+k} = S_t \exp\left(a\left(1 - S_t / \bar{S}\right)\right) \tag{4.11}$$

where R_{t+k} is the stock returning after k years, $\bar{S}$ is the stock size in natural equilibrium and S_t is the escapement of the cohort in year t producing the returning fish in year $t+k$. Measuring R and S in the same units, the returning fish will exactly replace their parent cohort when $S = \bar{S}$, so we may identify $\bar{S}$ as the natural equilibrium population.

The model is shown in Figure 4.11. The yield of the fishery depends strongly on the growth parameter a. The escapement (S) providing maximum yield also depends on the growth parameter a; the higher it is, the smaller the escapement producing maximum yield. The sustainable yield is the difference between the replacement line, where the run exactly replaces itself, and the recruitment function, and the maximum sustainable yield is identified by the dotted line tangential to the recruitment function and parallel to the replacement line. Cost considerations as well as time discounting would influence the optimal escapement in qualitatively the same manner as already discussed. This model can produce cyclical and even chaotic behaviour, depending on the growth parameter a. For $a > 2$, the natural equilibrium becomes unstable and displays cyclical behaviour; for sufficiently large values of a, these cycles become irregular and even chaotic. A sufficiently high exploitation rate could, in fact, stabilize a population that has a cyclical natural equilibrium.

If the growth parameter a is "moderate" – that is, not much larger than 1 – the fishery is likely to be initially characterized by large but unsustainable

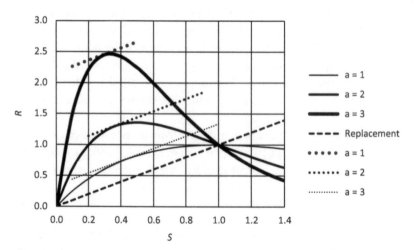

Figure 4.11 Ricker's recruitment curve

catches. If, with $a = 1$, the fish stock is initially reduced from its natural equilibrium of $S = 1$ to the one that maximizes the sustainable yield ($S = 0.4329$), the initial catch of fish would be $1 - 0.4329 = 0.5671$, but only 0.33 could be taken from the run produced by this optimal escapement. With $a = 2$ the corresponding numbers would be $S = 0.3608$ with an initial catch of $1 - 0.3608 = 0.6392$, but the run emerging from this optimal stock would yield a maximum catch of 0.9348.

Notes

1. To solve the infinite geometric series $S = kx + k^2x + \ldots$ when $k < 1$ we multiply it by k, getting $kS = k^2x + k^3x + \ldots$; subtract the latter series from the first, getting $S(1 - k) = kx$, because k^T approaches zero as T approaches infinity. From this we get $S = kx/(1 - k)$, or $S = x/r$, because, in our case, $k = 1/(1 + r)$.
2. The exceptions are sedentary species, such as oysters.
3. These rents are discussed at some length in Hannesson (1978).
4. This is often called the "skipper effect". See, for example, Bjarnason & Thorlindsson (1993).
5. These cases are analysed in Hannesson (2002).
6. Ulltang (1980) provides an early analysis of this problem.
7. This is the 2019 report by the ICES working group on Arctic fisheries (AFWG), available on ICES's website (ICES stands for International Council for the Exploration of the Sea, with headquarters in Copenhagen). This website (www.ices.dk) is an ocean of information on fish stocks in the Northeast Atlantic, as ICES is charged with giving management advice for fish stocks in this area.
8. This selectivity pattern was calculated as average age-specific fishing mortality from 2010 to 2019 divided by the highest age-specific fishing mortality. Source: ICES (2019a: tab. 3.15).
9. ICES (2019a) shows different numbers for the weight of fish in the stock and in the catches. We use weight in the stock, as reported in table 3.19 for forecasts for 2019, and estimate a von Bertalanffy growth function: $w_t = w_\infty \left(1 - \exp\left(-K\left(h - h_0\right)\right)\right)^3$. The parameter w_∞ shows the asymptotic weight of fish (fish that live on indefinitely), which comes out as 67 kg (the largest cod ever caught weighed 60 kg).
10. Beverton and Holt (1957), Ricker (1958, 1975). The specification here follows Pitcher and Hart (1982). In estimating the parameters of these curves it was assumed that the differences between observed recruitment and the values predicted by the curve are lognormally distributed, as most recruitments are well below average, with large recruitments occurring sporadically.
11. Note that the spawning stock is only a part of the entire stock, and for the maximum of the sustainable yield curve it is only 1.26 million tonnes, whereas the entire stock is 2.8 million tonnes. Maximum recruitment occurs for a spawning stock of 0.9 million tonnes.

5

NATURAL FLUCTUATIONS OF FISH STOCKS

In Chapter 2 we discussed the variability of fish catches and fish stocks at some length. Catches from some stocks have risen rapidly and then fallen just as rapidly to almost nothing (the Peruvian anchovy, the California sardine, the Japanese sardine). But after some time, decades in some cases, these stocks have bounced back and sometimes even surpassed their previous peaks. In this chapter we shall take a closer look at variations in fish stocks, in particular some other stocks that have collapsed. There are few if any cases of collapses without subsequent recovery, however, even though it may take a long time, even decades.

The variability of fish stocks can play out on several timescales. The shortest timescale is the year-to-year variability in recruitment – that is, variations in the size of fish cohorts. In temperate or cold waters spawning is seasonal; fish gather in their spawning grounds at a certain time of the year and may migrate hundreds of kilometres to get there (an example is the Northeast Arctic cod migrating from the Barents Sea to the area around the Lofoten islands). Each fish spawns millions of eggs, but most get eaten by other fish before they mature or die for other reasons. Small variations in an enormously high egg mortality could explain the large variations in cohort size. Suppose a fish spawns 70,000 eggs and that the normal mortality is 99.99 per cent. Of the 70,000 eggs only seven would normally survive. With a mortality of "only" 99.98 per cent, fourteen would survive, and the recruitment from that fish would be doubled.[1]

The variability in recruitment can also play out on longer timescales. First, there are the apparently irregular high peaks of recruitment; typically fish cohorts are below average size in terms of numbers, but every once in a while there is an exceptionally large recruitment, which sustains the fishery for many years to come. We shall see an example of this below, drawn from the Northeast Arctic cod stock. The causes of these variations are not well known. The availability of critical food at a critical time has been mentioned. Another possibility is variations in the abundance of fish preying on eggs and larvae. We will encounter one such case below when we discuss the variability of the Barents Sea capelin.

Second, there are long-term irregular cycles in the abundance of fish stocks. Stocks may persist with recruitment at a high, albeit variable, level for decades and then plummet to low levels with poor recruitment for a long period. We will encounter this phenomenon below as we discuss the history of the California sardine. The causes of these irregular cycles are not well known. In some cases they seem to be correlated with ocean temperature, but the fundamental reason is not necessarily the temperature as such but environmental factors correlated with it. When coupled with excessive fishing, the result of environmental conditions turning to the worse could be a collapse of the stock for longer or shorter periods of time, and it may be challenging to find out whether the collapse is a result of overfishing or adverse environmental effects. Below we shall discuss the cases of the Norwegian spring-spawning herring, the Northern cod of Newfoundland and the California sardine.

This variability poses problems for the fishing industry. Nowadays many fisheries are regulated by annual fish catch quotas, to be discussed in Chapter 8, but this does not mean that fish catches are stable from year to year. Fish catch quotas are set with reference to the state of fish stocks as they are estimated at the time the quotas are set (we shall shortly discuss one such "quota-setting rule" used for the Northeast Arctic cod). Fish quotas will therefore go up and down with the underlying fish stock, which causes problems for the utilization of fishing boats and for supplying fish markets. When fish stocks "disappear" for a decade or more, as has happened and we will see below, it causes painful restructuring in the industry; boats that used to fish a stock that vanished do not necessarily have another stock to go to, while the processing industry and retailers could find alternative sources of supply more easily, given modern transportation equipment and preservation methods.

Sustainability and variable stocks

The variability in stock abundance poses some difficult questions for sustainability. What is the sustainable yield of fish stocks with such enormous variability as the Japanese or the California sardine that we discussed in Chapter 2? Is the concept of sustainability at all applicable? If we define sustainable yield from a fish stock as a constant quantity that can always be taken from the stock without endangering its existence, this quantity could in some cases be very small and even zero. We would be forgoing substantial catch opportunities by following such a policy. A more reasonable approach is to adjust the catches taken in any given period to what the stocks can support at the time. This may imply large variations in fish catches, which in turn may over- or undersupply fish markets. A compromise may have to be reached between the stability markets demand and the catching opportunities fish stocks provide. Some flexibility is provided by the ability of fish processors and consumers to substitute one type of fish for another. Some of us are hooked on eating haddock, but we might be willing to put up with cod if haddock are rare and expensive. Fishmeal can be made from a variety of fish, and it makes relatively little difference where the meal comes from: capelin, blue whiting or anchovy.

A straightforward approach would be to define sustainability in terms of rates of exploitation, or what amounts to the same thing: rates of fishing mortality. As we saw in the previous chapter when discussing the Northeast Arctic cod, fishing mortality could be so high as to wipe out the mature part of the stock. Any level of fishing mortality below that level would avoid that trap, but the fish yield would be very small for high mortality rates. A constant and sustainable rate of fishing mortality would result in fish catches that vary together with the stock itself, but the exploitation would be sustainable in the sense of not leading to the disappearance of the stock in the long term. One of these rates would provide the maximum sustainable yield, defined as the maximum yield of fish per year over the long term. It is difficult to provide an exact definition of what a "long term" is, because fish stocks can be subject to "regime shifts" in the ocean; changes in environmental conditions, about which there is limited knowledge, can produce changes in the productivity of fish stocks.

In their advice to fisheries managers, fisheries scientists recommend fish catches such that a certain level of fishing mortality will not be exceeded. This need not be the mortality rate that produces the maximum sustainable yield over the long term; it is typically something less, for precautionary purposes. Furthermore, fisheries scientists often define certain "reference points" below which the spawning stock should not fall. If a stock is near such a reference point, fish catches should be cut back in order to avoid falling below that level. This may seem a bit strange, as the recruitment of fish seems virtually independent of the size of the spawning stock over a wide range. Everyone would agree, however, that no fish produce no fish, and small spawning stocks are unlikely to produce a good recruitment. The million-dollar question is: how large is the critical size of the spawning stock? Perhaps we should be happy not to have found that out.

An example of a "harvest control rule" of this kind is a recent one developed for the Northeast Arctic cod. The rule is shown in Figure 5.1, but is slightly more complicated.[2] The fishing mortality providing maximum sustainable yield is F_{msy} = 0.4. We see that this target mortality prevails over a relatively narrow range for the spawning stock. If the spawning stock falls below 460,000 tonnes the target fishing mortality is reduced proportionally with the spawning stock, and if it exceeds 920,000 tonnes it is increased proportionally to a maximum of F = 0.6. The reason for the latter is cannibalism; large cod eat

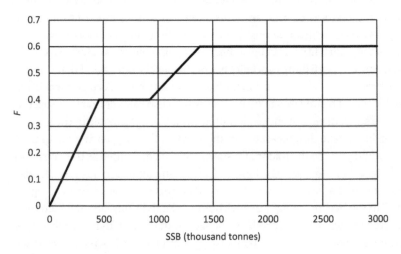

Figure 5.1 Harvest control rule for Northeast Arctic cod
Note: SSB = spawning stock biomass.

smaller ones, as mentioned in the previous chapter. Letting the fish survive beyond a certain age is counterproductive in terms of fish yield, partly because they have passed the age of maximum biomass, as discussed in Chapter 4, and partly because they eat younger, fast-growing fish of their own kind.

The Norwegian spring-spawning herring

The Norwegian spring-spawning herring is an interesting case, from the point of view of variability and sustainability. The stock has been exploited for hundreds of years, and there are time series covering more than 100 years of catches, estimated stock size and fishing mortality (Toresen & Østvedt 2000; Toresen *et al.* 2019). The stock spawns off the west coast of Norway. The fish larvae are carried by currents into the Barents Sea, where they grow up, and as the fish mature they migrate in search of food into the Norwegian Sea and towards Iceland. The stock used to be fished in large quantities in the summer and autumn off Iceland, even by Norwegians, because after feeding in spring and early summer the fish had accumulated fat – ideal conditions to produce spicy salted herring, a delicacy that the Swedes called Icelandic herring ("Islandssill") and purchased in considerable quantities. In the late 1960s the stock crashed and temporarily ceased its wide-ranging migrations.[3]

Figure 5.2 shows the recruitment and the spawning stock of Norwegian spring-spawning herring from 1907 to 2019 (recruitment is moved back two years because the recruits are two years old). There are, in particular, two things to note. First, there are some extraordinary high peaks of recruitment. This is typical of fish stocks, as we have already seen for the Northeast Arctic cod. Herring, like the Northeast Arctic cod, have a lifespan of more than ten years, so that a large year class is fished for several years.

Second, it is difficult to see any correlation between recruitment and the size of the spawning stock. The correlation coefficient for the shorter and more recent of the two data series in Figure 5.2 is in fact negative. For the older and longer series it is positive, 0.33, which is not high but significant (at the 5 per cent level). This is largely, but not solely, attributable to the period from 1968 to 1986, when the spawning stock was exceptionally small and produced small recruitments, with one exception. In 1983 the sixth largest recruitment on record since 1907 was produced by a very small spawning

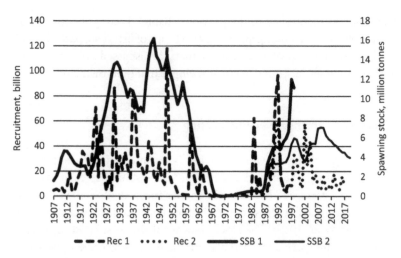

Figure 5.2 Spawning stock biomass (SSB) and recruitment (Rec) of Norwegian spring-spawning herring, 1907–2019
Note: Recruitment year t is moved to year t-2, to correspond to the stock that spawned it.
Sources: Toresen & Østvedt (2000), data series 1; ICES (2019b), data series 2.

stock. This was the beginning of the recovery of the herring stock. By 1990 it can be considered as having recovered to a "normal" level, but note that there is a difference between the two time series of the spawning stock; the older series shows a much larger total stock. This is because they are produced by two different methodologies, which broadly agree on time pattern but not on level.

This leads on to the third thing to note from Figure 5.2: the collapse of the stock in the late 1960s. The spawning stock declined over just a couple of years from more than 1 million tonnes to less than 80,000 tonnes. This is, not surprisingly, reflected in the catches; as Figure 5.3 shows, they fell from 630,000 tonnes to just 45,000 tonnes in 1968. The main reason for this precipitous decline was overfishing. Over just a few years prior to the collapse the fishing fleet went through a technological revolution that increased the productivity of the boats tremendously (Gordon & Hannesson 2015). The main change was the introduction of a mechanical winch, the so-called power block, which pulled in the seines used to encircle shoals of herring.

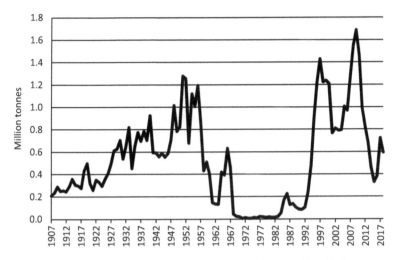

Figure 5.3 Catches of Norwegian spring-spawning herring, 1907–2018
Sources: Toresen & Østvedt (2000), ICES (2019b).

This made it possible to catch larger shoals and did away with the need to put small auxiliary boats on the water to encircle the herring shoals. The other innovation was the sonar, which made it possible to find the fish shoals underwater, whereas previously shoals would be detected as ripples on the surface or by putting out a line with a sinker and checking if the line would be displaced by a fish shoal underneath. This new technology resulted in a very high fishing mortality and, together with weak recruitment to the stock in the 1960s, almost wiped out the stock.

It has been debated whether the herring collapse could have been avoided. It has been pointed out that this occurred before the establishment of the exclusive economic zone, to be discussed in the next chapter. The herring were exploited by several nations bordering the Northeast Atlantic: Iceland, Norway, Russia, and others. The fishery was largely conducted outside national boundaries, which at the time were 12 nautical miles, so no nation had the authority to enforce fisheries regulations in this area. This is not an unreasonable explanation. To someone remembering these times, as this author does, it seems no less reasonable that people in the industry, and government officials as well, had not yet understood how powerful the new technology was; that it had advanced to the point of being able to destroy the herring stock if let loose. Fishing for herring used to be very hard work and the rewards uncertain; shoals of fish were difficult to find, and, once found, could be large enough to rip the seines asunder. Fisheries scientists prior to the sonar and the power block used to be popular for helping to find fish shoals and predict their behaviour, but their popularity vanished in the industry, at least for a while, as they became bearers of bad tidings: that the herring was mostly gone.

Ultimately the stock recovered, undoubtedly thanks to strict regulations that prohibited landings of small fish and amounted to a virtual moratorium. This was aided by the establishment of the 200-mile exclusive economic zone. The Norwegian zone was established in 1977, and by that time the herring had virtually become an exclusively Norwegian resource, having ceased their feeding migrations taking them hundreds of nautical miles away from the shores of Norway. As already stated, by 1990 the stock had returned to normal, whereafter it resumed its feeding migrations. These migrations take it into what remains of open seas outside national economic zones and into the exclusive economic zones of Iceland, the Faeroe Islands and Russia. The herring stock is now managed by these nations plus the European Union.[4] As Figure 5.3 shows, the catches after the mid-1990s have exceeded their earlier peaks, but they have gone up and down together with the stock. The herring fishery is now regulated by catch quotas set on the basis of advice from fisheries scientists, who recommend that fishing mortality not exceed a certain critical level.[5] The countries involved have often agreed on a total quota for catches from this stock and then divided it among themselves, but it has also, and rather frequently, happened that they disagree on both the total catch quota and its division. Nevertheless, it appears that the stock is fairly moderately exploited. We shall return to this issue in Chapter 7.

The Northern cod of Newfoundland

Another stock that has collapsed, primarily because of overfishing, is the Northern cod of Newfoundland. This stock resides off the northern coast of Newfoundland and southern coast of Labrador and was, until its collapse around 1990, the largest cod stock in the world. It used to be fished by fleets from several nations. The Basques were the pioneers. Then came the English, in the seventeenth century; the abundant cod fishery was the primary reason for the English colonization of Newfoundland. The French were also there, and the small islets of St Pierre and Miquelon, off the Newfoundland coast but still a part of France, are a legacy of the French fishery in the area. In modern times boats from Spain and Portugal are the main foreign fleets in the area, but otherwise Canadian boats dominate.

The collapse was sudden. As Figure 5.4 shows, the catches of Northern cod trended slowly upwards from 1850 to 1960, but with substantial year-to-year variations. Then, in the 1960s, came a sudden burst up to a record of over 800,000 tonnes in 1968. This was associated with the development of large trawlers, mainly in European countries (the Soviet Union and their satellites, West Germany, Britain), that could process their catch on board. This development affected other nations as well and was a major factor in the strife for extended national fishing limits, an issue we shall discuss in the next chapter. In the rhetoric of the moment, these fleets were accused of vacuuming the oceans clean of fish.

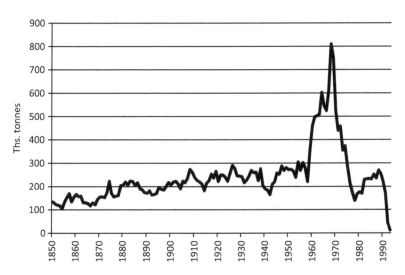

Figure 5.4 Catches of the Northern cod of Newfoundland, 1850–1992
Source: Ransom Meyers (personal communication).

In contrast with the Norwegian spring-spawning herring, the area where the Northern cod stock resides had largely been incorporated into a single national (Canadian) jurisdiction when it collapsed. The fishery was dominated by Canadian fishing boats, and the Canadian government had a high degree of control over the fishery. Some of the fishery did take place outside the Canadian exclusive economic zone, however, as the continental shelf, where the fish are located, protrudes outside the 200-mile limit. Nevertheless, the fishing was not limited in a timely enough manner that might have avoided the collapse. The fact that the fishery was the main provider of employment in towns and villages along the coast of Newfoundland was undoubtedly a factor; shutting the fishery down would have been unpopular and politically risky. Ultimately, it became unavoidable, and the fishery has largely remained closed ever since. The exception is a small-scale "sentinel" fishery, which partly has the purpose of gathering facts about the stock; is anything available out there? One would not know without trying.

Figure 5.5 shows the size of the spawning stock of Northern cod from 1983 to 2019, as assessed by Canadian fisheries scientists. The precipitous fall over just two years (1991 to 1993) is highly conspicuous. After 2005 there

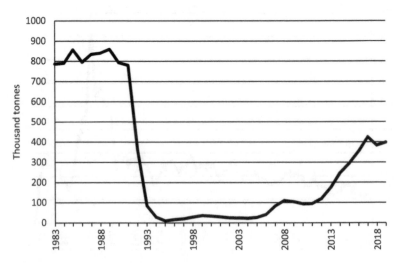

Figure 5.5 Spawning stock of Northern cod, 1983–2019
Source: Fisheries and Oceans Canada (2019).

has been some recovery, but the stock is still only halfway to its abundance in the decade before 1991. Since 2017 the recovery has come to what may be a temporary halt.

Fisheries scientists have debated whether the collapse of the Northern cod was caused by environmental factors or overfishing.[6] In the years prior to the collapse the waters where the Northern cod resides cooled appreciably. This led to slower individual growth. The spawning stock declined, and so did recruitment (Drinkwater 2002). Trawlers caught lots of small fish, which were thrown overboard because small fish fetched a lower price than larger ones; the trawler fleet was by that time under a regime of fish catch quotas, and it made little sense to fill them up with fish of low value. This generated higher fishing mortality than intended. One factor that may have contributed to the collapse is that the much-used production function we discussed in Chapter 4 (Equation (4.3)) did not hold. According to this equation, the catch per unit of effort is proportional to the stock size. The catch per unit of effort in commercial catches held up well despite a rapid decline of the stock, which has been attributed to stock density not falling in proportion to the stock. There is some evidence that the stock gathered in small "pockets" of warmer water as the sea became colder. This is where they were caught towards the end, when targeted fishing for Northern cod was banned in the summer of 1992.

This last point illustrates not only that fish stocks are subject to short-term fluctuations because of environmental changes on an annual scale, but that they are also subject to changes on a longer timescale, which may be several years up to decades. Such long-term changes are often characterized as "regime shifts" and are probably related to long-term changes in weather patterns or climate. An example of such weather patterns is the so-called North Atlantic oscillation, changes in the difference in atmospheric pressure in winter between the "Iceland Low" and the "Azores High". This affects the strength of the westerly winds in the North Atlantic and thereby the strength of the Gulf Stream bringing warm water to northwest Europe. But those strong winds also create an opening for cold winds and waters flowing from the Arctic to the coast of Labrador and northern Newfoundland. This is what happened in the years around 1990 (see Drinkwater 2002).

After this dramatic and sustained decline in landings from the major fish stock supplying the fishing industry in Newfoundland, one would have thought that the value of fish landings would fall correspondingly. Figure 5.6

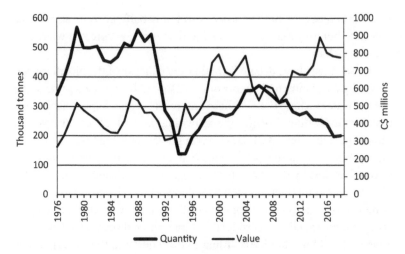

Figure 5.6 Quantity (thousand tonnes) and value (million Canadian dollars at 2018 prices) of fish landings in Newfoundland, 1976–2018
Source: Fisheries and Oceans Canada.

shows a different picture. The value of fish landings picked up quickly from a moderate decline between 1987 and 1992, and so did even the quantity landed. What happened was a substantial increase in landings of valuable crustaceans. Figure 5.7 shows the landings of shrimp and queen crabs in Newfoundland from 1990 to 2018, together with the size of the spawning stock of Northern cod. It is striking how the landings of shrimp and crabs began to rise shortly after the collapse of the Northern cod fishery, and also how they have declined after the recovery of the cod stock. There are two, not necessarily competing, theories about what may lie behind this. First, cod eat shrimp and probably small crabs as well, so these species will thrive if the cod stock is brought down. Second, the environmental factors that are adverse for the cod stock may promote the growth of shrimp and crabs.

These comments about what has happened to cod, shrimp and crabs off the coast of Newfoundland over the last 30 years alerts us to the notion of ecosystem management. Creatures in the ocean are interrelated; one species feeds on another: zooplankton feeds on phytoplankton, small pelagic fish such as herring and capelin feed on zooplankton, cod feed on small pelagics

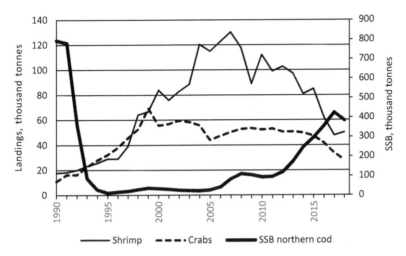

Figure 5.7 Landings of shrimp and queen crabs in Newfoundland and the spawning stock of Northern cod, 1990–2018
Source: Fisheries and Oceans Canada.

such as capelin, and seals feed on cod and other fish. It is popular to talk about the food chain and ecological levels, but things are more complicated than that. The same species of fish feeds at different ecological levels over its lifetime; cod fry feed on zooplankton, but larger cod feed on other fish, including their own kind. One could envisage directing the captures of fish at different levels of the food chain so as to maximize the provision of food from the sea. This would entail catching fish at a low level in the food chain, because 80 to 90 per cent of the biomass is lost through transfer from one level to another. But fish at a low ecological level are, typically, not very tasty; neither anchovy nor capelin is a popular food fish. Therefore, one might wish to maximize the value of food extracted from the ocean. Having capelin pass through the stomachs of cod may lose 90 per cent of the biomass, but increase the value of fish consumed by an order of magnitude or more. Therefore, we should not necessarily eliminate the predators and fish at the lowest possible level in the food chain in order to avoid a loss of biomass in transfers between different levels. The problem reminds us of the discussion of aquaculture in Chapter 3: does it make sense to have feed fish pass through the stomachs of salmon? From an efficiency point of view, yes, if consumers are willing to pay sufficiently more for the salmon than the feed fish, and for some feed fish there is no consumer demand at all.

The feeding relationships in the sea are probably not well enough known to practise this kind of ecosystem management on a grand scale. Smaller-scale management along these lines is not unknown, however; we shall touch upon this again when we discuss the capelin fishery in the Barents Sea later in this chapter. But the notion of ecosystem management seems to be most popular in circles that regard life in the sea as something other than a source of food and material benefits, advocating limiting captures of small pelagic fish such as sardines and anchovy so as to support populations of seabirds and seals, as we touched upon in Chapter 3. There may indeed be "demand" in certain circles for fish for that purpose, but it seldom translates into transfers of money. Moreover, by accommodating this demand we would be satisfying lofty immaterial benefits at the expense of material food supplies and the livelihood of fishermen.

The California sardine

In the 1930s and 1940s the California sardine supported one of the largest fisheries not just in the United States but the whole world. Figure 5.8 shows the landings in California and the size of the stock from 1929 to 2018.[7] In the 1940s and 1950s both the stock and the landings declined steeply, despite a short recovery around 1950, and in the early 1960s the fishery was stopped. The stock decline was initially blamed on overfishing. Later research, however, has indicated that in the past, and long before any fishing began, the sardine stock has been subject to cycles of crashes and recoveries (Baumgartner, Soutar & Ferreira-Bartrina 1992). Overfishing thus need not have been the sole cause of the decline of the sardine stock in the 1930s and 1940s; it might have declined in any case due to natural reasons, as it apparently has done periodically in the past and now again in very recent years.

For over 20 years (from 1965 to 1988) the catches of sardine in California were negligible, less than 1,000 tonnes per year. The stock is believed to have been very small; the data series operates with a nominal value of 5,000 tonnes. Around 1990 a targeted fishery was permitted again; the stock exceeded

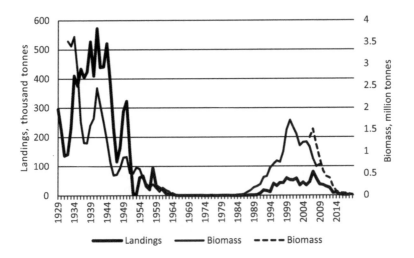

Figure 5.8 Biomass (age 1 and older, 1932–2019) and landings (1929–2018) in California of California sardine
Sources: CALCOFI database, 1929–2009; Hill, Crone & Zwolinski (2019), data since 2006.

100,000 tonnes, and it grew rapidly from there to more than 1.5 million tonnes, comparable to what it was in the early 1940s. But the fishmeal and canning industries were gone, and the sardine catches permitted after the recovery around 1990 have been nothing like what they used to be in the past; they reached a peak in 2007 of 81,000 tonnes, 15–20 per cent of what they had been in the heydays around 1940.

Since 2007 the sardine stock has declined continuously, and in 2019 it was estimated at just about 20,000 tonnes. The sardine catches in California have been correspondingly reduced, and in 2018 stood at just under 2,000 tonnes. As of 2019 the directed sardine fishery in California was closed and the small quantity caught used as live bait (Hill, Crone & Zwolinski 2019: 26). The recent collapse of the sardine stock could be attributable to natural variability, even if earlier this century the landings were comparable to what they were around 1940. The fishery in California is only a part of the whole; the sardine is also fished in Mexico, and, as Figure 2.8 shows, the total landings exceeded 700,000 tonnes in some years after the turn of the century. What drives the environmental "regime changes" affecting the sardine is not entirely clear. Jacobson and MacCall (1995) demonstrate a positive correlation between ocean temperature and recruitment to the sardine stock, but the recent collapse has coincided with the highest temperatures for over 100 years, as measured by the Scripps Oceanographic Institute in San Diego.

The Barents Sea capelin

The Barents Sea capelin fishery developed in the wake of the collapse of the Norwegian spring-spawning herring around 1970. The fishmeal industry in Norway needed a new source of raw material and the fishing fleet a new stock to exploit. The capelin stock was insufficient to keep all the fishing fleet employed, however, and inaccessible for the smallest boats.

Figure 5.9 shows the stock and catches of Barents Sea capelin from 1972 to 2019. We can divide this period into two phases: before and after 1985. Before

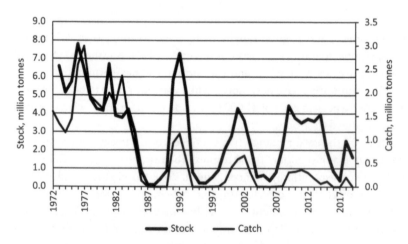

Figure 5.9 Stock and catches of Barents Sea capelin, 1972–2019
Note: Stock numbers refer to 1 October and are moved to the next year to better correspond to the year of captures.
Source: ICES (2019a).

1985 the stock fluctuated substantially, but never fell below 3 million tonnes. The catches fluctuated correspondingly, being regulated by a catch quota that took an increasing share of the available stock.

After 1985 the stock fluctuations increased in magnitude, and there have been several periods when the stock has been below 200,000 tonnes. When the stock has been below 1 million tonnes, no or very small catches have been permitted. Years with zero catches are thus not a sign of a stock collapse but the result of careful management, in order to avoid a collapse of the spawning stock. The capelin is a fish with a short lifespan; most of them die after spawning, and they rarely reach an age of five years. It is thus not possible to smooth the catch pattern over time through saving a part of a large capelin stock for later capture, as one can do, to a certain extent, with a stock composed of several year classes, such as the cod. Whatever is available in good years must be taken there and then, and the industry will have to live with the resulting fluctuations in catches or forgo them altogether. Note that such highly variable catches can be eminently sustainable, provided the fishery is closed down when the fish stock is in poor shape.

The reason the capelin stock never fell below 3 million tonnes in the years from 1972 to 1985 is believed to be the small herring year classes at that time. The immature year classes of Norwegian spring-spawning herring drift up north to the Barents Sea, where they grow and mature. These young herring feed on capelin larvae, so that, if there is a lot of herring around, the stock of capelin is decimated. Figure 5.10 shows the total biomass of Barents Sea capelin and the biomass of one- and two-year-old herring in the Barents Sea. There are strong signs of a negative correlation, but there is one cycle in which a large stock of capelin coincides with a large biomass of young herring (the years around 2000).

Cod are major predators of capelin in the Barents Sea. In their present stock assessments, fisheries scientists take into account expected predation by cod when making recommendations on the catch quota for capelin. This may be taken as an example of ecosystem-based management.[8] It is noteworthy, when we compare Figures 5.10 and 5.11, that the stock size of capelin has trended down since 1990 while the catches of cod have trended up. The increased catches of cod are the result of an increase in the cod stock. A larger stock of cod means increased predation pressure on the capelin.

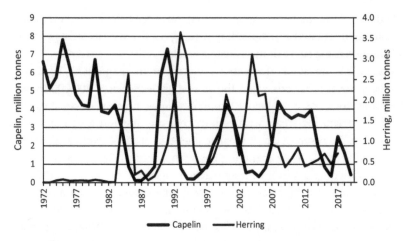

Figure 5.10 Total biomass of Barents Sea capelin, 1972–2019, and the biomass of one- to two-year-old herring in the Barents Sea, 1972–2017
Source: ICES (2019a).

Inter-annual variability and long waves

As we have seen, fish stocks vary on both long and short timescales. These long-term variations need not be as severe as high abundance followed by near-disappearance. We round this off with examples from two North Atlantic cod stocks: the Northeast Arctic cod and the Iceland cod. The catches from both stocks have declined significantly over long periods, but even at their low points they have still been substantial.

Figure 5.11 shows the recruitment and catches of Northeast Arctic cod. The variability of recruitment is enormous: the largest year classes are more than ten times larger than the smallest ones and they occur both irregularly and infrequently; most year classes are below average. A few years after the exceptional year classes have been recruited they are fully accessible to the fishery, and fish catches peak for a few years and decline after that. We see this particularly clearly in the 1950s, 1960s and 1970s. There were three large year classes in a row from 1951 to 1953, and catches peaked very markedly about four years later, from 1955 to 1957. Two large year classes were recruited in 1966 and 1973, and the catches duly peaked from 1968 to 1970

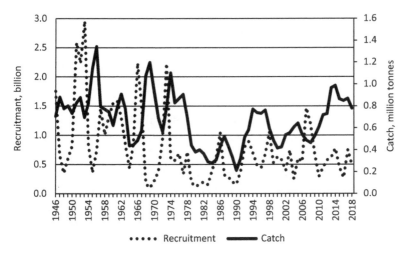

Figure 5.11 Recruitment (billion individuals) and catches (million tonnes) of Northeast Arctic cod, 1946–2018
Source: ICES (2019a).

and again from 1974 to 1977. After 1974 the exceptional year classes have become markedly smaller, and in recent years there has been a longer period between peak recruitment and peak catches; the large year classes recruited in 2007 and 2008 generated peak catches six years later, in 2013 and 2014. This is probably the consequence of a changed pattern of selectivity in the fishery, discussed in the previous chapter; the fishery now captures fish a little older than used to be the case. There is obviously a strong serial correlation in recruitment, producing short-term irregular cycles of six to ten years' duration.

We can also notice a long wave in the fishery. In the first 30 years, from 1946 to 1975, the catches often exceeded 1 million tonnes. Between 1976 and 1992 they hardly exceeded half a million tonnes and fell to a low point of just over 200,000 tonnes in 1990. The years around 1990 were crisis years, and gave the impetus to fish quota regulations in the fishery – an approach discussed in Chapter 8. Since that time the catches have trended upwards, reaching almost 1 million tonnes in 2013 and 2014. This is probably attributable both to better management (lower fishing mortality) and a more benign ocean climate; in recent years the ocean temperature in the northern seas where the stock resides has been higher than ever before since measurements began to be taken early last century.

The remark on selectivity illustrates the fact that the effects of peak recruitment can be accentuated or smoothed by changing the selectivity pattern of the fishery. If the selectivity is sharp, taking fish at the age of maximum biomass, and the fishing mortality is high, the recruitment peaks will a few years later produce sharp peaks in fish catches. If selectivity is gradual and proceeds to a peak over many age groups of fish and the fishing mortality is low, the large recruitment will increase fish catches over many years, for fish stocks with a long lifespan such as the cod. There is thus a trade-off between large but infrequent peaks in catches and more even catches over time, involving some sacrifice of the large peaks for avoiding the deep troughs in between. It is not unlikely that marketing considerations, and perhaps also utilization of the fishing boats, favour sacrificing the peaks for more even catches.

The cod stock at Iceland is smaller than the Northeast Arctic cod; peak catches have rarely exceeded half a million tonnes. Figure 5.12 shows the catches of cod at Iceland from 1905 to 2019. We see a similar pattern of peaks and troughs as we did for the Northeast Arctic cod, and they are generated by the same kind of mechanism: variations in recruitment with exceptionally large recruitment occurring irregularly. There are some other patterns worthy of note. First, we see deep troughs in catches during the two world wars in the previous century; foreign fishing fleets largely disappeared from Icelandic waters during both wars. After the two wars we see high catch peaks, which probably are a result of the decline in fishing mortality during the absence of foreign fleets, building up a stock that then could be "mined" in later years. During the first half of the last century foreign fleets took more than a half of the cod catch at Iceland.

Another thing to note is the disappearance of foreign fishing fleets in the late 1970s. This was the consequence of the "new law of the sea" emerging in that period: the establishment of the 200-mile exclusive economic zone, which we shall discuss in the next chapter. Most of the cod at Iceland is found within 200 miles of shore, so foreign fishing fleets could be denied access to the stock on the basis of national jurisdiction within the 200-mile exclusive economic zone.

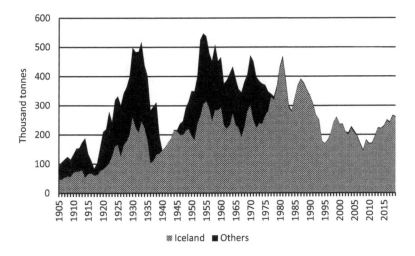

Figure 5.12 Catches of cod at Iceland, 1905–2019
Source: Marine and Freshwater Research Institute, Iceland: www.hafogvatn.is.

The third point to note is the declining trend in fish catches, from the peak of 550,000 tonnes in 1954 to a trough of 150,000 tonnes more than 50 years later (2008). Why this happened is not well known. It could be a result of changing ocean climate: in the 1950s and 1960s the stock at Iceland used to be augmented by fish migrating from Greenland, but these migrations ceased as the stock at Greenland went into decline in the 1970s. Since 2008, however, the trend in fish catches has been strongly upwards.

Notes

1. Based on an example for haddock given by Pitcher & Hart (1982: 105, 174).
2. See the 2019 report of the ICES working group on Arctic fisheries (ICES 2019a: 126).
3. There was also a stock of spring spawners residing at Iceland, which seems to have become extinct as a result of the overfishing in the late 1960s. See Óskarsson (2018).
4. This was the pre-Brexit situation. At the time of writing (summer 2020) it is not clear what Brexit will mean for the management of the herring.
5. The current management strategy, agreed in 2018, is a fishing mortality of $F = 0.14$ when the spawning stock is above 3.184 million tonnes. For lower values, F is to be reduced linearly to 0.05 at a spawning stock of 2.5 million tonnes (ICES 2019b: 170).

For comparison, F_{msy} = 0.157 according to the same source (*msy* stands for maximum sustainable yield).

6. For a summary of this, see Drinkwater (2002). A paper strongly emphasizing overfishing is Hutchings & Meyers (1994).

7. The data series are discontinuous at year 2009. The data for 1929 to 2009 come from the CALCOFI database, accessed in 2010 (the biomass data begin in 1932). The later series begins in 2006 and shows a similar trend. It comes from Hill, Crone & Zwolinski (2019).

8. This is summarily described in ICES (2019a: 522).

6

THE 200-MILE ZONE: A SEA CHANGE

We have in previous chapters seen why fisheries have to be controlled: fish catches must be limited in order to avoid fish stock collapses, fishing mortality must be limited in order to maximize long-term yields, and the selectivity of fishing gear must be controlled in order to take advantage of fish growth or smooth fish catches over time. Any such control requires jurisdictional authority, first to set the rules and regulations and then to ensure that they will be followed, ultimately applying the powers of the sovereign state to punish violators as needed to deter infractions.

This mechanism works best within the borders of the sovereign state; the same state apparatus then sets the rules and punishes the violators. But fish stocks move about in the sea and are not easily kept within the limits of any single state. Many, and possibly the majority, of the stocks migrate between the waters of two or more states, and some into international waters where no state has jurisdiction except over boats flying their flag. There are even stocks that reside in international waters over their entire lifespan. Fisheries regulations, therefore, often require agreements between different states, none of which has power to impose regulations in the entire area where the stocks will be located over their lifespan. The enforcement of rules, including such as may have been agreed with other states, is much easier within a state's jurisdiction, however, than on the high seas outside the boundaries of any state.

In this chapter the development of the international law of the sea will be traced, from its freedom of the seas stage to the exclusive economic zone that is the premise of modern fisheries management. It is a fascinating story with unexpected twists and turns and, like all political sausage-making, not necessarily the perfect one for achieving optimal results. Be that as it may, the arrangement we currently have has necessitated wide international cooperation in fisheries management, some of which is formalized in regional management fisheries organizations given a somewhat special status by a fisheries agreement under the auspices of the UN.

A brief history of the modern law of the sea

The history of the modern law of the sea begins with the great discoveries in the 1490s. In their wake, the two Iberian maritime superpowers at the time, Spain and Portugal, met to reconcile their interests. This resulted in the Treaty of Tordesillas in 1494, so named after the place where the meeting was held. The treaty divided the world into two spheres of interest. Portugal was to have the Indian Ocean and the Atlantic Ocean to a line that in a modern frame of reference lies about 46°30′ west of Greenwich, and Spain the rest. We see traces of this today; Brazil, colonized by the Portuguese, is largely east of the said meridian, Spanish-speaking Latin America west of there.

But the emerging seafaring powers of northwest Europe, the Netherlands and England, would have none of that. They wanted freedom to trade with countries in what the Portuguese and Spanish claimed as their exclusive area, especially in spices, so valuable at the time. The Dutchman Hugo Grotius wrote a treatise supporting this claim, entitled *Mare liberum*, which roughly translates as *The Freedom of the Sea*. Grotius wrote in Latin, as any European intellectual worthy of respect did at the time (his book was published in 1609). The subtitle was less lofty and went straight to the point: *De ivre qvod Batavis competit ad Indica*, which roughly translates into *On the Right the Dutch Have to Compete in India*. The "competition" referred to the spice trade, and "Batavia" is the Latin name for the Netherlands.

In Grotius' view, no country could claim exclusive rights over territory which it could not defend. Another Dutchman, Cornelis van Bynkershoek, took Grotius' argument further and argued that a strip that could be defended from land could therefore be claimed as a part of the sovereign territory. An Italian, Ferdinand Galiami, estimated the range of the most effective cannon at the time to be three nautical miles. The cannons improved, but the three-mile rule stuck and proved amazingly resilient. It is a good example of a simple rule that survives because it serves a purpose, even if the original reason for it has disappeared or become patently invalid. We will see other such examples in our short discussion of the law of the sea.

The three-mile rule suited the British Empire perfectly. Over time it evolved into a trading colossus, with interests in every nook and cranny of the world. The trade was built on navigation; this was long before aeroplanes had even been thought of. And Britain also developed a fishing fleet that operated in distant waters: the Barents Sea, at Greenland, Iceland, the Faeroe Islands, Canada (Newfoundland), and elsewhere. It was imperative for a fleet such as that to have as free access to fish resources as possible, something the three-mile limit provided. The British therefore promoted the three-mile limit as best they could and managed for a long time to make it into an accepted norm in international law. International law, by the way, is not set by a legislative assembly and signed by a "world leader"; it consists of written and informal agreements that sovereign states find in their interest to follow. It goes without saying that empires and powerful nations have a large influence on what becomes "accepted international law", and so did the British Empire in its heyday.

But there were exceptions. Norway was unhappy with the three-mile rule, which followed the coastline, meaning that wide fiords and bays were open for foreign fishing boats. It claimed fishing limits of four nautical miles and also a right to close off fiords and bays by drawing straight lines across them, and issued legislation to this effect in the 1930s. Britain took the case to the International Court of Justice in The Hague, which in 1951 ruled in Norway's favour. This was to have repercussions in Iceland, which in the 1950s made claims to extended fishing limits. In 1952 Iceland closed off fiords and bays and claimed a fisheries jurisdiction of four nautical miles.

But other international developments were afoot that undermined the three-mile rule. In 1945 US president Harry Truman issued two proclamations that had a deep and lasting effect on the law of the sea. One, the more important, was about territorial rights on the ocean floor. In previous years oil extraction offshore in the Gulf of Mexico had been developing and expanding further and further out. The Americans wanted these resources for themselves, and President Truman issued a proclamation claiming sovereignty over the resources on and in the continental shelf, the boundaries of which at that time were usually set at a depth of 200 metres. The continental shelf is, as the name suggests, an extension of the land mass, but that extension typically ends at a depth of about 200 metres, and then the ocean bottom falls off steeply to a much greater depth. The other proclamation by Truman, of lesser consequence, was that the United States asserted the right to set up special protection zones for fishing, but without claiming national ownership of the fish resources. This distinction vis-à-vis the oil industry may well have been rooted in the fact that the United States was engaged in distant-water fishing, especially for tuna, and may not have wanted to create a precedent for claiming national ownership over fish stocks.

Other countries with different interests did not want to make a distinction between resources on and underneath the continental shelf and the fish swimming in the sea above. One was Iceland, which claimed ownership to fish stocks over the continental shelf. The demersal fish stocks at Iceland – cod, haddock and saithe, all of them important – are largely confined to the Icelandic continental shelf. Argentina and Mexico made similar claims, speaking about the "patrimonial sea".

But the countries on the west coast of South America – Chile, Peru and Ecuador – had different interests. The continental shelf of these countries is very narrow, and they exploited fish species located close to the ocean surface and over depths of more than 200 metres, such as anchovy (Chile and Peru) and tuna (Ecuador). They were not satisfied by using the continental shelf as a criterion and wanted a more extensive, geographical one. The Chileans blew the dust off an earlier proposal they had developed in the early 1940s for extending their offshore jurisdiction in order to protect their whaling industry. They had developed a new method for processing whale oil and wanted protection for their whaling against the fleets from Europe – British and Norwegian – which they expected would return after the war. The Chileans asked their lawyers for advice, and the lawyers looked for precedence, as lawyers do, and found nothing better than the hemispheric protection zone set up on the initiative of the United States for the protection of marine transportation against belligerent actions by the warring nations of Europe. This protection zone varied in extent, but on an impressionistic map published in early 1940 it looked as if it might be 200 nautical miles or so. This was the germ of the 200-mile exclusive economic zone.[1]

The Chileans got support for the 200-mile limit from Peru and Ecuador, and all three declared a 200-mile wide national jurisdiction at sea in the late 1940s.

For many years they were alone in making such extensive claims, but there was a strong undercurrent for extending jurisdiction at sea to 12 nautical miles. Two conferences on the law of the sea under the auspices of the UN were held in 1958 and 1960, and they almost succeeded in getting the stipulated two-thirds majority for fishing limits of 12 miles, but with exemptions for those who traditionally had fished within this area. A six plus six-mile limit had the largest following, where fishing history would be respected within an outer belt of six miles.

After the second UN conference more and more nations declared a 12-mile-wide national fishing zone, or even full jurisdiction. Iceland and the United Kingdom had a dispute about this in 1958, known as the cod war, when British trawlers fished under the protection of the Royal Navy. The conflict was resolved in 1960 with some concessions to the British. But the world moved on, and there was an increasing tendency towards extending fisheries jurisdiction at sea, not least because of the development of new and effective trawlers that could catch large quantities of fish in a short time period. We touched upon this in Chapter 5 in connection with the Northern cod of Newfoundland. Then, in 1973, the UN began its third conference on the law of the sea, which ended up labouring on for nine years, though not continuously but in intermittent sessions. What held it up for long was disagreement about deep-seabed mining, which to this day struggles to get going because of the high costs involved. On fisheries, however, there was near-consensus already in 1973 about extended jurisdiction to 200 miles. The Chileans had managed to sell their 200-mile idea to the group of developing countries, which, incidentally, included many landlocked states with little interest in jurisdiction at sea. But this was the time of worries about resource scarcity, of resource nationalism and of pushes by newly independent poor countries to take full control of their resources. Most rich countries, particularly in Europe, did not initially support the 200-mile idea, which made it all the more appealing to the poor and newly independent countries. Eventually it was the United States, on an initiative by Congress, that jumped the gun and declared a 200-mile-wide exclusive fisheries zone – exclusive, that is, for its own boats. Many other countries, Norway and Canada among them, established a 200-mile exclusive economic zone in 1977, long before the third UN conference on the law of the sea was officially over. In fact, the conference ended as a formal failure; several countries, including the United States, refused to endorse the

Convention on the Law of the Sea, which the conference proposed and was meant to be accepted by all. This has not prevented the Convention from becoming international law, however, both through widespread adoption of its stipulations and by a large majority of the countries of the world ratifying it.

The 200-mile exclusive economic zone, as defined in the Convention on the Law of the Sea, gives coastal states jurisdiction of resource use in the zone, but not jurisdiction over things such as the passage of ships. The jurisdiction over resources covers both fish and resources on and underneath the seabed; for the latter there are special provisions in case the continental shelf extends further than 200 miles. The fact that such provisions do not extend to the fish has produced conflicts and disagreements in many cases. The Grand Banks are located on the continental shelf of Newfoundland and protrude outside the 200-mile limit, where cod and other fish stocks are accessible to foreign fleets, mainly from Europe. The Canadians have complained that these fleets – or, rather, the governments of the countries they come from – have been uncooperative in cutting back fishing as necessary to save the fish stocks, the Northern cod being one of them. In the early years of this century Icelandic trawlers began to fish cod in the so-called "Loophole", an area in the Barents Sea outside national jurisdiction. The episode caused consternation in Norway and Russia, because they were trying to rebuild the Northeast Arctic cod stock from its low point in 1990 (see the previous chapter). This episode, now resolved, is a good example of how countries take a stand on issues of principle on the basis of their interests. Iceland, having got what it wanted by the 200-mile zone, was beginning to fish in distant waters, a practice it previously had been against. Yet another problematic area is the so-called "Donut Hole" between the United States and Russia, where there is a portion of the ocean surrounded by the 200-mile jurisdiction of these countries. Valuable groundfish stocks such as Alaska pollock are accessible in this area.

As these examples illustrate, the 200-mile exclusive economic zone does not cover the entire world ocean; the distance between countries and continents often is a good deal more than 400 nautical miles. Figure 6.1 shows roughly how much the 200 miles cover. Note that this pertains to potential coverage; there are still unresolved boundary issues in various parts of the world. Two of these are in East Asia and involve China: there is the issue of the Spratly Islands and the Paracel Islands in the South China Sea, where China claims areas that are also claimed by Vietnam and the Philippines; and, further north,

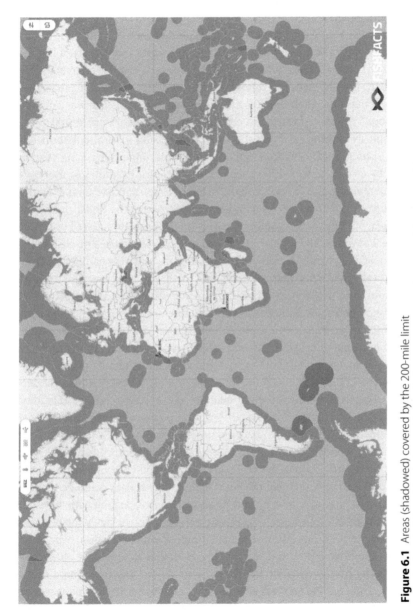

Figure 6.1 Areas (shadowed) covered by the 200-mile limit

Note: The "Loophole" is visible northeast of the border between Norway and Russia, and the "Donut Hole" at the eastern end of the map.

Source: Courtesy of Óli Samró (Samró 2016).

there are the Senkaku (Japanese), alias Diaoyu (Chinese) Islands, claimed by China and Japan.

A glance at Figure 6.1 gives the impression that the 200-mile limit covers only a minor part of the world oceans. In terms of area this is correct, but the productivity of the oceans differs widely. The most productive areas are on or close to the continental shelf; this is where most of the world's fish catches are taken. At the time when the 200-mile zone was established, it was believed that about 5 per cent of world fish catches came from areas outside 200 miles, but it quickly became clear that this was an increasing share and that uncontrolled fishing outside national jurisdiction could undermine conservation efforts by coastal states within their 200-mile zones. Examples of this have been mentioned: the "Loophole", the "Donut Hole" and the Grand Banks. Therefore, the UN organized yet another conference, in the 1990s, on the law of the sea, but one that focused exclusively on the problems related to fishing outside 200 miles. The official name was the UN Conference on Straddling Fish Stocks and Highly Migratory Fish Stocks. This unwieldy name came from the efforts by the United States to distinguish between tuna, in which it had an interest in distant-water fishing, and other migratory stocks, in which it had little or no interest, or perhaps the opposite interest. There are certain nearly contradictory articles in the Convention on the Law of the Sea that stem from this distinction. After three sessions over three years the conference resulted in an agreement on these types of stocks, one usually referred to by the shorthand title of "the UN Fish Stocks Agreement". Interestingly enough, the Fish Stocks Agreement did not take the logical step of further extending coastal state jurisdiction but, instead, empowered so-called regional fisheries management organizations to manage fisheries outside the 200-mile limit.

One may wonder why the UN conference on migratory fish stocks did not proceed further along the way staked out by the UN conference on the law of the sea that had ended ten years earlier. One reason could be that the conference on fish stocks was a one-issue conference, dealing with access to stocks outside 200 miles. A compromise between different views and interests pertaining to that issue is not evident; perhaps an extension over short distances, perhaps some fudging making it look as if access for all nations is still being preserved while the fishing outside the limit is brought under control. The solution agreed whereby the regional fisheries management organizations are empowered to deal with fisheries outside 200 miles has some elements of the latter. By contrast, the third UN conference on the law of the sea was a multi-issue conference; everything was on the table: access to resources, navigation of straits, seabed mining, and more. It has been alleged that the two superpowers at the time, the United States and the Soviet Union, gained navigation rights and access to straits while giving in on access to the fish. But the United States gained handsomely from extending its limits, and was in fact one of the first countries to do so, while the Soviet Union lost most of its distant fishing waters.

The impact of the 200-mile zone

The 200-mile zone was a sea change, literally and metaphorically. Fish stocks that do not migrate outside 200 miles – and there are many of those – became, in effect, the property of the coastal state establishing jurisdiction over the area where they reside. A country that has full jurisdiction over the area where its fish resides can maximize its return from its fisheries without needing to negotiate measures about their management with any other country. This would normally entail that the fish stocks be protected against depletion, to ensure a continuing flow of benefits from exploiting them. Running down stocks for a short-term gain would make sense only in exceptional circumstances, such as when the discount rate of the future is extremely high, the growth rate of the fish is extremely low or there is a non-negligible probability that the stock will vanish for purely natural reasons. Nevertheless, there is still ample scope for conflicts between different user groups or industry segments over the allocation of fish quotas when a single country has full control in principle, as we shall discuss further in Chapter 8.

But, even in cases when stocks migrate between two or more countries, the chances of good management emerging through international cooperation are much improved. Provided the stocks do not straddle into the high seas, the number of governments that can claim an interest in a migratory fish stock is limited. No third party can in that case undermine agreements between the given number of parties within whose exclusive economic zones the fish migrate. It is very different in the cases when fish stocks migrate into the high seas, the area outside the fishing limits of any state. As already stated, the UN Fish Stocks Agreement gives the authority to manage fish stocks in this area to regional fisheries management organizations. One weakness of this arrangement is that there is no limit on the number of countries with a legitimate claim to resources in this area except the number of countries in the world with a coastline. This makes it more cumbersome to reach agreement on management. In some organizations, a consensus is required for agreements; in others, a qualified majority. These organizations can be expected to have greater difficulties in agreeing on management measures the larger and more diverse their membership. In the following chapter we shall further discuss the prospects for international cooperation on fisheries management.

A second problem for these organizations is that they have no jurisdiction on the high seas; no one has jurisdiction in this area except flag states over their own boats. Not surprisingly, it was foreseen that the enforcement of fisheries regulations on the high seas would be problematic. Therefore, the UN Fish Stocks Agreement includes articles on inspecting fishing boats on the high seas that are suspected of fishing in contravention of fisheries regulations in this area. A state that is a member of a regional fisheries management organization has a right to board and inspect a boat from another state that need not be a member of the organization. There are elaborate and cumbersome requirements regarding how this is to be done. If there is evidence of wrongdoing, the flag state is to be notified, as the flag state and no other has jurisdiction on the high seas. It is up to the flag state what countermeasures are to be taken, and one can doubt both the ability and the willingness of the flag state to do so; in fact, the near- or total absence of anything such is the very reason there are so-called flags of convenience. This is very different from the procedures within a country's exclusive economic zone; a boat where there is evidence of violating fisheries agreements can be promptly taken to harbour in the coastal state concerned and the captain taken to court and, together with the owner, sentenced to whatever penalties are appropriate. Flag states may delegate their jurisdiction to coastal states, however.

To overcome the substantial obstacles in the way of enforcing fisheries regulations on the high seas, the regional fisheries management organizations have resorted to blacklisting fishing boats caught violating their regulations. These lists are open information and shared between the different organizations involved in management on the high seas. Such boats are supposed to be sanctioned; not to be able to sell their fish catches, not to be able to obtain provisions or necessary service in any port and not to be licensed for fishing by any other fisheries management organization. Member states would seem to be obliged to enforce such sanctions; but transhipments at sea are one way of avoiding this. It bears noticing that inspecting alleged violators at sea is done by enforcement vessels that are meant to guard the economic zone of their own home state but that venture into the high seas for enforcement purposes as well. This is not a cheap operation, and countries would most likely have a stronger incentive to police their own exclusive economic zone than the high seas, where they share the benefits of fishing with many others.

The blacklists of violators on the high seas make for interesting reading. The impression is that these activities are declining, rather than the opposite, but there could be many cases that have not been discovered. The blacklists contain information about the owner and the flag state; in the majority of cases both are listed as unknown. To complicate matters further, the reflagging of boats is easy.

To compensate for the difficulties of enforcing fisheries regulations on the high seas, procedures have been developed to deal with boats engaged in illegal, unreported and unregulated (IUU) fishing, to be followed by the states in whose ports such boats seek to land their fish or obtain provisions or services. Under the auspices of the FAO, an agreement on procedures for port states was approved in 2009 and entered into force in June 2016, 30 days after the date of deposit of the 25th instrument of adherence. Known as the Agreement on Port State Measures, it is the first binding international agreement that specifically targets IUU fishing. It lays down a minimum set of standard measures for parties to apply when foreign vessels seek entry into their ports or while they are in their ports. As of 2019 the agreement had 63 parties, but the fact that there are continuing conferences on the issue indicates that there still is some way to go before the IUU problem can be considered solved.[2]

Regional fisheries management organizations

The FAO lists more than 60 "regional fisheries bodies" on its website, which also provides basic information on what they do. Not all of these are management organizations, in the sense that this is where the countries concerned meet, negotiate and eventually sign agreements on catch regulations and other things related to fisheries management. Some of the organizations listed are purely advisory, or perhaps lobby organizations. The International Council for the Exploration of the Sea (ICES) is an umbrella organization for fisheries biologists from countries around the North Atlantic, and in the North Pacific area there is a similar organization popularly known as PICES (Pacific ICES). ICES organizes meetings for fisheries biologists and is charged with giving advice to governments on fisheries management, but the management issues themselves, the appropriate catch quotas and their allocation between the countries concerned are resolved, or not resolved, in other organizations explicitly tasked with such issues. The North Atlantic Salmon Conservation Organization, for example, works for limiting catches of salmon in the open sea to support stocks in rivers in Iceland, Norway and elsewhere.

The organizations dealing directly with management cover either certain types of fish or geographical areas. The Northeast Atlantic Fisheries Commission covers fisheries in what is left of the high seas in the Northeast Atlantic irrespective of fish species. So does its sister organization, the Northwest Atlantic Fisheries Organization. The International Commission for the Conservation of Atlantic Tunas has a self-explanatory name, and so does the Pacific Halibut Commission, set up by the United States and Canada a long time ago. Tunas are highly migratory, and there are regional organizations dealing with tunas in all three major oceans.

Løbach *et al.* (2020) provide an up-to-date overview of the world's fisheries management organizations, which is accessible on the FAO website. They make a distinction between organizations dealing with regional fisheries management, as provided for in the UN Fish Stocks Agreement, and other types of organizations. The former are directly involved in adopting fisheries management measures such as setting quotas for fish catches, regulating fishing gear or fishing days, or whatever is deemed necessary to ensure the sustainability of fish stocks. Many of these were established in this century or in the 1990s, in response to the UN Fish Stocks Agreement, but some are much older and usually have a mandate for certain species (tuna, Pacific halibut) and have been adapted to the new realities of the law of the sea. Løbach *et al.* (2020) list and discuss 22 organizations operating on the basis of the mandate from the UN Fish Stocks Agreement. Most of these organizations have a large membership, a reflection of the fact that fishing on the high seas is open to everyone. The record is held by the International

Commission for the Conservation of Atlantic Tunas, which has no fewer than 52 members. How many members there are is presumably an important determinant of how easy it will be to agree, or how ambitious any signed agreement will be, as will be discussed in the next chapter.

The wealth transfer of the 200-mile zone

In eighteenth-century England, vast areas that used to be common pastures or fields shared in an intricate system of rules were enclosed and turned from common property into a private one. It was a controversial process; it made some richer and others poorer; but there is little doubt that it made English agriculture more productive.[3] The enclosures enriched those who enclosed their land; this was, needless to say, the driving force behind the process. There are parallels with the establishment of the 200-mile zone; it made vast stretches of the ocean into domains of coastal states and may be seen as the biggest enclosure movement ever. This enriched coastal states in general, but at the expense of those states that used to fish in waters distant from their shores. There were clear dividing lines in the disputes in the previous century over fishing limits; those that stood to gain were for extension and those that stood to lose were against, and tried, first, to preserve the three-mile limit, and, as that case was lost, to limit further expansion as much as possible. As will be argued in Chapter 8, this enclosure movement of the oceans laid the foundation for more effective management of world fisheries, with nations acting in their self-interest just like the English owners of the enclosed farms, and simultaneously creating greater wealth by better management.

Paradoxically, perhaps, many of the states that gained most territory from the 200-mile limit were not those that used the fish resources in these waters most intensively. Under the old regime of the freedom of the seas, the technologically most advanced nations built fleets for fishing in distant waters, sometimes catching fish that those who lived in close proximity did not have the means to catch. The English pioneered trawling for fish at Iceland and in many other places. Most other coastal countries in Western Europe developed fishing in waters far from home; France, Belgium, Germany, Spain and Portugal all did so. The Japanese went far and wide in the Pacific fishing tuna. Coastal states such as Iceland, Canada, the United States, Norway and many others wanted extended fisheries jurisdiction so as to chase away foreigners and have the fish for themselves, yet there are many coastal states that made huge territorial gains from the 200 miles but, traditionally, took little or none of the fish in those waters. The most glaring examples are the Pacific island nations, which in some cases got a 200-mile-wide circle around a tiny speck of an island. They are sparsely populated and did not traditionally catch much fish except near the shore, but some of them lie astride the migratory routes for valuable tuna. Nations that traditionally caught tuna in these waters had to come to terms with these island states if they wanted to continue catching fish in what had become the national domain of these island states. Even if a sizable part of the Pacific Ocean remains outside the boundaries of any state, it is often preferable to have access to tuna fishing within the 200-mile zones. The Pacific island states lost little time in declaring their 200-mile exclusive economic zone. As early as 1978 Japan concluded the first agreement on access to the new zone with some Pacific island states, and the United States did so a bit later (1987). The European Union also has access agreements with the Pacific island states, but much of the EU member states' distant-water fishing occurs elsewhere, mainly off West Africa. In 1980 the European Union concluded access agreements with Guinea-Bissau and Senegal, and in subsequent years with a multitude of states in West Africa. These agreements are not primarily about tuna; they mainly relate to other fish, particularly shrimp and cephalopods.[4]

These access agreements are about payment in exchange for the right to fish. Originally these payments took the form of cash payments and involved both governments and the fishing companies. The government in the distant-water fishing country would pay the government of a coastal state, a Pacific island state or a coastal country in West Africa or elsewhere. This often took the form of foreign aid and was not necessarily formally attached to fishing rights. Then the fishing companies would pay for the right to fish, either a fee per tonne or a fee per boat or for a day fishing. Either way, there was a transfer of money, and there is no doubt that the coastal states involved gained from their new extended jurisdiction, even if not in the form of utilizing the fish resources themselves. One source quotes gains from access fees ranging from zero to over 30 per cent of GDP for the Pacific island states (Havice 2010).[5] The highest percentages relate to Kiribati and Tuvalu, both of which are poor.

Opinions are divided about the fairness of these gains. Some point out that these arrangements imply rich countries paying poor countries and that the sums involved are probably a lot less than the pure profits of the fishery. Others wonder whether geographical location alone is a good reason for entitlement to fish resources around the coasts; many coastal countries still do not much engage in fishing these resources themselves. Many, and perhaps most, aspire to do so, being plagued by lack of work opportunities and low incomes. It has turned out to be difficult to establish a fishing industry or a fish-processing industry in many of these countries, however. In some of them, most "domestic" boats are ones that have been reflagged from distant-water fishing nations and are still owned by companies or persons residing in the latter countries. Industrial processing facilities onshore are typically owned by foreigners.[6] Deficient infrastructure and communications are often obstacles to establishing fish processing in coastal states that traditionally have done little fishing in their waters. Boats equipped with up-to-date technology to catch fish in demand in rich countries are expensive; a modern tuna purse seiner costs upwards of US$25 million, according to a source from 2007, and they have not become any cheaper since then (Barclay & Cartwright 2007).

One weakness alleged to be associated with access agreements is weak enforcement. The coastal countries that have not developed an industry able to utilize the resources within their jurisdiction typically are in that position because they are poor and underdeveloped. For the same reason, they are not in a good position to enforce whatever agreements they might enter into with distant-water fishing nations. The agreements themselves have also been deficient from the point of view of limiting the amount of fish that the distant-water fishing nations are allowed to catch; there are not necessarily any limits on the total catch, but only limits on the number of boats and the time they can be used. Often these countries do not get any reports on how much fish the distant-water fleets have caught, and therefore lack the basic statistics to make any assessment of the fish stocks within their boundaries, even if they had competent scientists to do that kind of work. It would be bold to assume that the distant-water fishing nations have strong incentives to monitor their own fleets. The length of the time horizon they are operating within can be called into question; access agreements are limited in time, and it can be doubted whether they will be renewed. There has in fact been a certain change in the composition of distant-water fishing nations since the 200-mile limit became established. The United States, Japan and the European Union were the main players to begin with, but new players such as South Korea, Taiwan, the Philippines and China have been gaining ground. The latter ones, and China in particular, are different from the earlier players in that they sell their fish on the world market and not only on their own markets; China exports approximately half its catch to high-income countries (Chesnokova & McWhinnie 2019). The rise of China as a distant-water fishing nation has been rapid. In 1985 the China National Corporation had 13 boats fishing in West Africa. Today China has the largest distant-water fleet in the world; a relatively recent source cites 1,989 boats operating in 35 countries (Mallory 2013).

It goes without saying that the 200-mile zone will not facilitate any improvement in fisheries management if the coastal states leave the fishing in their zone to distant-water fishing nations and do not conclude clear and enforceable agreements that ensure sufficient conservation of the fish stocks. In such cases the 200-mile zone is likely to mean the opposite of conservation, namely a more rapid depletion of fish stocks. The distant-water fishing nations are likely to have a shorter time horizon than a coastal state acting in its own interest, as access agreements are of limited duration and new candidates for distant-water fishing could very well develop, just as the actors that recently arrived in this league did themselves.

Nevertheless, the absence of a domestic fishing industry does not need to be an obstacle to improved fisheries management within the 200-mile zone. The Falkland Islands have a large exclusive economic zone, being islands at considerable distance from the continent of South America. There are only a few thousand people living in the islands, and they have never engaged in fishing on any significant scale. The 200-mile zone gave them rich fish resources which they rent out to other nations' fleets to fish (some boats are owned by Falklanders but manned by foreigners). The revenue from the fisheries have substantially increased the public revenue of the islands and made them much less dependent on transfers from the United Kingdom's central government. The government of the islands has an obvious interest in maintaining the productivity of its fish stocks, and to that end it hires fisheries scientists with state-of-the-art knowledge to analyse fish stock data and requires the fishing fleets to provide sufficient information on their catches to make that possible.

Notes

1. This story is told in somewhat greater detail in Hannesson (2004).
2. As of 2020, the most recent was the one held in Santiago in June 2019, the minutes of which can be found at www.fao.org/3/ca5757en/ca5757en.pdf.
3. On the English enclosures, see Gonner (1966 [1912]).
4. Much has been written on access treaties; see, for example, Havice (2010), Barclay & Cartwright (2007) and Kazcynski & Fluharty (2002). A very brief but recent overview is provided by Chesnokova & McWhinnie (2019).
5. The numbers are from 2003.
6. Havice (2010), who also mentions that formal ownership records often are not available.

7

INTERNATIONAL FISHERIES MANAGEMENT: COOPERATION OR COMPETITION?

To effectively manage fish stocks, cooperation between nations is obviously required when the stocks migrate between the economic zones of different countries. Such cooperation is likely to be most demanding when stocks also migrate into the high seas, both because the number of nations with a legitimate claim is not clearly defined and because jurisdiction on the high seas is in the hands of the state where the boat is registered. In this chapter, we shall look at the scope for international cooperation in the light of a branch of economics known as game theory. This deals with the interaction between players when the actions of one player have a perceptible influence on the outcome for another. This is highly relevant for fisheries issues, as the outcome for one country depends on what other countries fishing the same stock might do. The name "game theory" may appear frivolous, but the subject is deadly serious; the amount of fish that one country decides to take out of the sea may have great consequences for what other countries can take in the future. Therefore, the amount of fish that one particular country decides to take in any given period has to be decided on the basis of what others are likely to do and how they are likely to react to what that particular country decides to do.

The setting is often illustrated by the famous "prisoner's dilemma". Two delinquents are suspected of armed robbery, but the police don't have any evidence. The two are put each in his own cell without the possibility of communication. They are made an offer. If one of them confesses and the other does not, he who confesses will be released, and the other one will be in jail for nine months. If both confess, they will be in jail for six months. If neither confesses, they will be in jail for a month because they were caught in a stolen car.

The outcome of the game can be illustrated by the following payoff matrix. The first entry in each cell is the outcome for player one, the second entry is the outcome for player two and the numbers are months in jail, negative since this is a negative payoff (after Gibbons 1992).

		Player two	
	Actions	*Confess*	*Deny*
Player one	*Confess*	−6, −6	0, −9
	Deny	−9, 0	−1, −1

If player two confesses, the best player one can do is to also confess; six months in jail is better than nine. If player two denies, the best thing player one can do is to confess; being released immediately is better than spending a month in jail. In this case, confessing is always the best strategy for player one, regardless of what player two does. This is also the best strategy for player two, because his payoff matrix is exactly the same as for player one. Therefore, both end up in a worse situation than they could have been in if they had cooperated and kept their mouths shut; spending just one month in jail is better than spending six.

One thing to note is that, in this setting, both players are kept isolated and without the ability to communicate. If they had been able to talk to each other, they might have vowed not to betray each other, though that raises the question whether they really could trust each other. Furthermore, they are not able to observe what the other one is doing; neither one of them knows what the other is doing or has done. This setting is very different from what we are dealing with in fisheries policy; countries can observe each other's behaviour and make the necessary moves if their partners are not fulfilling their obligations or are making moves that are threatening. This seriously limits the relevance of settings in which players, in this case countries, make their moves simultaneously without communicating or being able to observe what the others are doing.

One further thing may be noted about the prisoner's dilemma game. If both prisoners confess, they get a lesser reward than if the other one had chosen not to confess. It is this structure that ensures that the most attractive strategy for one player in isolation is to confess, irrespective of what the other might do. If the police had promised release in exchange for confession irrespective of what the other might do, our focal player would have been indifferent between confession and denial in case the other player denies.

The prisoner's dilemma setting is not entirely irrelevant in the context of international fisheries cooperation, however: it identifies the best possible reply to whatever other players might do. This is very useful to know, as it identifies the worst of all possible worlds, which one would presumably want to avoid through negotiation. And it could also help to support a negotiated outcome, given that defectors from that agreement could expect a reply along lines suggested by the worst of all possible worlds. The players we have in mind are individual countries fishing stocks that migrate between their economic zones or on the high seas, with the growth and future state of the stocks depending on how much they decide individually to fish in any given year.

Consequences of unfettered competition

Let us go back to the biomass model we presented in Chapter 4. Equation (4.3) related the catch of fish (Y) to fishing effort (E) and the size of the exploited stock (S):

$$Y = qES$$

Suppose now there are two countries, labelled 1 and 2, fishing the same stock. Suppose they are both equally efficient, so that they have the same q parameter. In this case we can simply dispense with it and set $q = 1$, because we can always measure E in units that make $q = 1$ without affecting the results. So, for the two countries we have

$$Y_1 = E_1 S \tag{7.1a}$$

$$Y_2 = E_2 S \tag{7.1b}$$

If we concentrate on a sustainable fishery, the amount that the two countries fish must be equal to the surplus production $G(S)$.[1] Using the logistic function (Equation 4.1), we get

$$\left(E_1 + E_2\right)S = aS\left(1 - S/K\right)$$

Solving for S, we get

$$S = K\left(1 - \frac{E_1 + E_2}{a}\right) \tag{7.2}$$

Inserting S into (7.1) gives

$$Y_1 = \alpha E_1 - \beta\left(E_1^2 + E_1 E_2\right) \tag{7.3a}$$

$$Y_2 = \alpha E_2 - \beta\left(E_2^2 + E_2 E_1\right) \tag{7.3b}$$

where $\alpha = K$ and $\beta = K/a$.

Now suppose that each country tries to maximize its sustainable yield. Each country has no control over the other country's effort and so could be expected to choose its own effort to maximize its own yield, for a given effort exerted by the other country. Mathematically, this means taking the derivative of (7.3a) with respect to E_1 and putting it equal to zero, and doing the same for (7.3b) and E_2. From this we get

$$\frac{dY}{dE_1} = \alpha - \beta\left(2E_1 + E_2\right) = 0 \tag{7.4}$$

and, solving for E_1,

$$E_1 = \frac{1}{2}\left(\frac{\alpha}{\beta} - E_2\right) \tag{7.5}$$

For country 2 we would get an analogous solution, which we drop.

Clearly, the effort exerted by country 1 to maximize its sustainable yield depends on E_2, the effort it expects the other country to exert, but cannot do anything about. What would make sense for country 1 to assume about this? Since both countries are equal, it would make sense for country 1 to assume that country 2 will exert the same effort. Putting $E_2 = E_1$ in (7.5) gives

$$E_1 = \frac{\alpha}{3\beta} = E_2 \tag{7.6}$$

What would the total sustainable yield be? Summing Equations (7.3a) and (7.3b) gives

$$Y = Y_1 + Y_2 = \frac{2}{3}\frac{\alpha^2}{\beta} - \beta\left(\frac{2\alpha^2}{9\beta^2} + \frac{2\alpha^2}{9\beta^2}\right) = \frac{2}{9}\frac{\alpha^2}{\beta} \tag{7.7}$$

How does this compare with the situation when there is only one country fishing? The term E_2 would drop out of (7.5) and we would have $E_1 = \frac{\alpha}{2\beta}$. From (7.3a) we would get, with $E_2 = 0$,

$$Y = Y_1 = \frac{1}{4}\frac{\alpha^2}{\beta} \tag{7.7'}$$

We see that the sum of the maximum sustainable yields for the two participants is smaller than the overall maximum sustainable yield. What happens is that the competition between two participants that do not coordinate their actions for the common good results in an overexploitation of the fish stock. The stock level is driven below the S_{msy} level and the yield is eroded.

We can derive a more general result showing how the result from competition gets worse and worse as the number of countries increases. Suppose "country 2" is in fact a collection of $N-1$ identical countries, N being the total number of countries including the one we are looking at. Substituting E_2 in Equation (7.5) by $(N-1)E_1$ gives

$$E_1 = \frac{\alpha/\beta}{1+N} = E_2 = ... = E_N \tag{7.6'}$$

Summing the yields for all countries gives

$$Y = Y_1 + ... + Y_N = N\frac{\alpha^2/\beta}{1+N} - \beta\left(N\frac{\alpha^2/\beta^2}{(1+N)^2} + N(N-1)\frac{\alpha^2/\beta^2}{(1+N)^2}\right)$$

$$= \frac{N}{(1+N)^2}\frac{\alpha^2}{\beta} \tag{7.7''}$$

The reader may check that this agrees with what we previously got for one and two countries.

Figure 7.1 shows how the total yield and the stock change with the number of identical countries when each tries to maximize its own yield, making rational assumptions about how much effort the other countries are going to

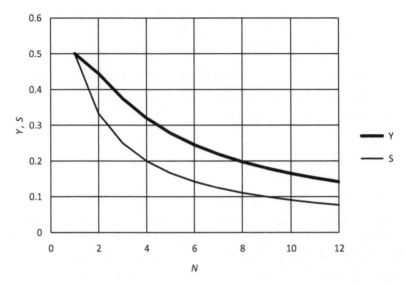

Figure 7.1 Yield and stock when each of N countries tries to maximize its yield from a fish stock with logistic growth with parameters K = 1 and a = 2

exert. We see that the yield falls quite rapidly below maximum as the number of countries increases (the maximum sustainable yield would be obtained with just one country), and the stock also falls rapidly below the maximum sustainable yield level.

If the unit cost of fish caught depends on the stock size, a single country controlling the stock would not go for the maximum sustainable yield but something less, and the stock would be above the *msy* level. It would then take more countries than otherwise to knock the stock below that level. On the other hand, countries might discount the future, which would imply a smaller optimal stock. None of this would greatly affect the main conclusion so far, that competition between several countries for maximum yield or maximum profit would lead to an overexploitation of the stock, both in a biological and an economic sense.

This conclusion is essentially the same as the one made famous by Garrett Hardin (1968) and usually called the "tragedy of the commons". In Hardin's narrative, shepherds graze their animals on a common pasture. Each shepherd is concerned only about fattening their own animals and cares little what happens to others. This leads to overgrazing, and all the animals return skinnier than they would be if there had been fewer of them. What matters for the individual shepherd is how much weight their additional animal might gain; they care little if that animal eats grass that animals owned by others might have taken. The tragedy lies in the overgrazing, and possible destruction, of the common pasture. This is exactly analogous to what happens in our fishery example.

Hardin has been criticized, and not without reason, for conflating two different concepts: common property and open access (see Frischmann, Marciano & Ramello 2019). Common property is shared between a limited number of individuals, either by custom, law or practicalities of access. Open-access resources are open to exploitation by anyone. Fish stocks that migrate between the economic zones of a limited number of countries are the common property of those countries, and, if they agree on how to manage them, that is all it takes; an outsider cannot lawfully send his boats into another country's economic zone and start fishing. Fish stocks on the high seas were a prototype of open-access resources; boats from any nation could fish such stocks if their owners found it worthwhile, and many did so from a long distance, even if distance was to some degree a hindrance for fishing just anywhere on the high seas. It is less clear whether fish stocks in what remains of the high seas are still under open access. Fishing on the high seas is still open to any country, but countries are supposed to fish in accordance with rules set by regional fisheries management organizations, as discussed in the previous chapter. It is still unclear how effective these organizations are in dealing with those that do not follow their rules, however. If some users of an open-access resource agree on its management, such agreement can always be challenged by parties outside that agreement, and that is all the more likely to happen if the agreement is successful.

The distinction between common property and open-access resources is crucial in principle. Elinor Ostrom made a name for herself, and earned the Nobel Memorial Prize in economics, for her work on common-property resources.[2] She found that, in many cases, users of common-property resources were indeed able to cooperate on their management and avoid the "tragedy of the commons". Nevertheless, despite the principal difference between common property and open access, there need not be much diffe-rence in practice; if common-property resources are shared between many, agreements will be difficult to attain and such resources could become overexploited as if under open access.

The conclusion so far is that competition leads to bad outcomes: overfishing, and possibly extinction, of fish stocks. This in fact we have already seen in Chapter 4, where we contrasted unmanaged fisheries with optimally managed ones. This may sound paradoxical to an economist; a central tenet in eco-nomics is that competition is a good thing, as it brings the consumer a greater volume of products, and better-quality ones and at a lower price. But we are talking here about competition for a finite resource, the productivity of which can be harmed by overexploitation, be it grass on the ground or fish in the sea. This is fundamentally different from processes that can be replicated and improved in quality, such as a new factory building more and better cars or assembling better computers. Competition is neither good nor bad in itself; under the right circumstances it works wonders, but under the wrong circumstances it can be utterly destructive.

The scope for cooperation

We have established that competition between countries to take as many fish as possible from a common fish stock is destructive. Agreement and cooper-ation would give a better result. Consider Figure 7.1 and the numbers that it shows. The maximum sustainable yield is 0.5. With 12 countries, the max-imum shown in the figure, the share of each would be 0.0417 if they limited their fishing effort to what is needed to take the maximum sustainable yield. When each tries to maximize its own yield, the total yield is 0.1420, with each getting only 0.0118. Clearly, there are gains from cooperation. More gener-ally, we can compare Equation (7.7'), which shows the maximum sustainable yield, and Equation (7.7"), which shows the sustainable yield when each of N countries tries to maximize its own sustainable yield:

$$\frac{1}{4}\frac{\alpha^2}{\beta} > \frac{N}{(1+N)^2}\frac{\alpha^2}{\beta} N \geq 2$$

Suppose cooperation has been agreed. Since this is an agreement between sovereign states, it must be such that each party to the agreement finds it in its own interest to honour it. There is no international enforcement mechanism that can be brought to bear on sovereign states except by their own assent. So what about the incentives to follow the agreement? It depends on how far-sighted the states are. Any single country could increase its catch of fish by increasing its fishing effort, provided that the others stick to the effort they had agreed to. But that is unlikely to happen. Seeing that one country cheats is likely to provoke similar behaviour in others, because their catches of fish would decline on account of the cheating country's behaviour, and a way to compensate for that would be to do likewise. The countries would end up in the competitive equilibrium, with each getting 0.0118 instead of 0.1420 under the agreement. Realizing that this would happen, the cooperative solution could prevail as a far-sighted equilibrium; despite short-term gains for defectors, all would be worse off in the end.

This draws our attention to the possibility that the viability of a cooperative solution depends on how countries value short-term gains in relation to long-term losses. This depends partly on the discount rate and partly on how diluted the losses are: does a country that abandons cooperation carry most of those losses itself, or are they mostly borne by others? The more diluted the losses are, the stronger the incentive to abandon cooperation. To demonstrate this, suppose N identical countries are fishing on a common stock in an area that is open to all. We take the same approach as we did in Chapter 4 and assume that the fishing occurs by periods and that the stock in the beginning of each period t, R_t, depends on how much was left after fishing in the previous period, S_{t-1}:

$$R_t = S_{t-1} + G\left(S_{t-1}\right) \qquad (7.8)$$

In the cooperative solution, the countries have agreed to leave behind an economically optimal fish stock, S^o, and fish the sustainable yield from that stock, $G(S^o)$. The price of fish and the cost of fishing are determinants of the economically optimal stock. We assume that all these parameters are the same for all countries involved (differences could, of course, lead to disagreements and thwart cooperation). The optimal stock and its sustainable yield will produce a profit per period of $\pi^o(S^o)$. If cooperation prevails for ever, the present value of profits for each country will be[3]

$$V^o = \frac{\pi^o\left(1+r\right)}{rN} \tag{7.9}$$

where r is the discount rate.

Now suppose that one of the countries breaks the agreement and continues fishing after the stock has been fished down to the agreed level S^o. Instead, the country fishes down the stock to a level S^*, which, in order to maximize short-term benefits, will be equal to the level at which no further fishing in the current period is profitable. This would be zero if the cost per unit of fish caught is independent of the stock level, but positive otherwise. Suppose the deviation is not discovered, or cannot be retaliated against, until the fishing period is over. But in future periods the other countries will do likewise, provided the stock has not been wiped out; this is the best response they can make to the deviant country's actions. The stock level S^* will produce a profit $\pi^*(S^*)$, the present value of which, for each country, is

$$V^* = \frac{\pi^*\left(S^*\right)}{rN} \tag{7.10}$$

Note that this flow of profits begins after the period of deviation, one period later than (7.9).

Breaking the cooperative agreement will be profitable if

$$V^* + D > V^o \tag{7.11}$$

where D is the profit the country gets in the period it deviates from the cooperative agreement. This is

$$D = \frac{\pi^o\left(S^o\right)}{N} + T\left(S^o - S^*\right) \tag{7.12}$$

In the first part of the period of deviation the deviating country gets its share of the cooperative profit, π^o/N. In addition, it gets a transitional benefit T from fishing down the stock from S^o to S^*. This accrues solely to the deviating country. Using Equations (7.9), (7.10) and (7.12) we can write (7.11) as

$$T\left(S^o - S^*\right) > \frac{\pi^o\left(S^o\right) - \pi^*\left(S^*\right)}{rN} \tag{7.11'}$$

which has a straightforward interpretation: the once-and-for-all transitional gain (T) must be greater than the present value of the difference between the cooperative and non-cooperative profits from the period after deviation onwards. Note that a high discount rate and a large number of participants make this difference small. For large enough r and N, it is possible that the transitional gain will outweigh the long-term loss; the transitional gain is not shared with anyone, whereas the loss is shared between all. The number of countries can therefore be critical for maintaining a cooperative solution. Another thing worthy of note is that a cooperative solution can always be maintained by a low enough discount rate; as r approaches zero the right-hand side of (7.11') approaches infinity. With a low enough discount rate, transitional gains are always dwarfed by losses over an infinite period.

Migrating stocks

The outcome of fisheries negotiations between nations depends on how the fish migrate between their economic zones. There are several possibilities. A stock might spawn in a certain location in a particular country's economic zone and then move to the zones of other countries, and the eggs and larvae might drift in the same fashion. This is the case for the Northeast Arctic cod, which spawn around the Lofoten islands in the Norwegian zone, and then migrate to the Spitzbergen area and into the Barents Sea and partly into the Russian economic zone. The eggs and larvae drift in the same fashion. Then there are the North American salmon, which leave the rivers where they were spawned, spend several years in the ocean and then head back to their "home" rivers and are fished on their way. On their return journey they might pass either through American or Canadian waters even if their destination is a river in British Columbia or in Washington state. This has certain features in common with herring, mackerel and blue whiting in the Northeast Atlantic. Blue whiting and mackerel spawn west of the British Isles in winter and then migrate towards Norway and into the North Sea, passing through the economic zone of the Faeroe Islands on their way. Some of the fish migrate towards Iceland, and in recent years into the Greenlandic economic zone. Norwegian spring-spawning herring spawn off the Norwegian coast in winter and migrate towards Iceland in spring and summer, passing through the Faeroese economic zone on their way. Some of these fish migrate into the banana-shaped area that is left of the high seas between Norway, Iceland and Greenland (see Figure 6.1).

The split stream model, which we are about to discuss, was developed with North American salmon in mind, but it might fit the situation for some other migrating stocks reasonably well. In the split stream model, a stock of fish, X, migrates from a common growth area to the economic zone of two countries in the fixed proportions β and $1-\beta$ (this can be extended, of course, to more than two countries, and the shares could be made variable and uncertain).[4]

Suppose now that each country wants to maximize the present value of its fishery over an infinite time horizon. Ignore fishing costs, or, more appropriately, assume that the cost per tonne of fish caught is a constant and that the price is also constant, so we can express value with a net price p of fish. We start with a stock X_0 given by history, which we can do nothing about, migrating to the economic zones of the two countries in the fixed proportions mentioned above. We assume that the fish stay in each country's area while they are being fished. Each country can then leave behind an amount of fish S that maximizes the present value of its fishery and that will be the same in all periods, as long as no economic and technological parameters change. The stock left after fishing goes back to the common growth and breeding area, and a replenished stock then migrates to the zones of the two countries in the next period. This is a simplification of reality; typically, individual fish grow while the stock is being fished. Formally, we can pose the problem as follows:

$$\text{Maximize } V_1 = p(\beta X_0 - S_1) + \frac{p}{r}\left\{\beta\left[S_1 + \bar{S}_2 + G\left(S_1 + \bar{S}_2\right)\right] - S_1\right\} \quad (7.12a)$$

$$\text{Maximize } V_2 = p((1-\beta)X_0 - S_2) + \frac{p}{r}\left\{(1-\beta)\left[\bar{S}_1 + S_2 + G\left(\bar{S}_1 + S_2\right)\right] - S_2\right\}$$

$$(7.12b)$$

The first term in these equations is the value of the catch of fish in the first period; the catch of fish is simply the difference between the amount of fish migrating into each country's zone and what it leaves behind; the two countries are labelled 1 and 2. The last term is the present value of the fishery from the second period onwards, as this is a convergent geometric series with a finite value even if the series is infinite (see footnote 1 in Chapter 4). The surplus growth (G) depends on the total amount of fish left after fishing in both countries' zones. We have put a bar over S_2 in the problem for country 1, and vice versa for country 2, because this is a given for country 1; country 1 has no control over how much fish country 2 leaves in its own zone.

To find the amount of fish (returning stock) that the two countries leave behind after fishing, we take the derivative of the two expressions:

$$\frac{\partial V_1}{\partial S_1} = -p + \frac{p}{r}\left\{\beta\left[1 + G'\left(S_1 + \bar{S}_2\right)\right] - 1\right\} \leq 0$$

$$\frac{\partial V_2}{\partial S_2} = -p + \frac{p}{r}\left\{(1-\beta)\left[1 + G'\left(\bar{S}_1 + S_2\right)\right] - 1\right\} \leq 0$$

where the prime (') denotes the derivative of the growth function with respect to the stock left behind after fishing. We can rewrite these equations as

$$G'\left(S_1 + \bar{S}_2\right) \leq \frac{1+r}{\beta} - 1 \qquad (7.13a)$$

$$G'\left(\bar{S}_1 + S_2\right) \leq \frac{1+r}{(1-\beta)} - 1 \qquad (7.13b)$$

The surplus growth function (G) is valid for the stock as a whole and common for both countries, so obviously Equations (7.13a) and (7.13b) cannot both hold with strict equality simultaneously. If we identify country 1 as the major country ($\beta > \frac{1}{2}$), the right-hand side of (7.13b) will always be larger than the right-hand side of (7.13a). What this means is that country 2 will always want to leave behind a smaller stock than country 1. Figure 7.2 shows a situation in which Equation (7.13a) holds with strict equality and where $G'(S)$ is the derivative of the growth function (the slope of a tangential line to the curve) at the stock level S_1°, assumed to be optimal for country 1. Country 2 would want a smaller stock than country 1; it would want a situation in which a steeper line is tangential to the surplus growth curve. The only situation that could prevail is one in which country 2, the smaller country, leaves nothing behind and Equation (7.13b) holds with strict inequality.

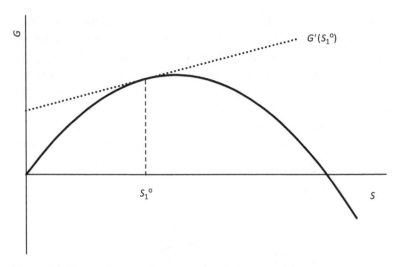

Figure 7.2 The surplus growth curve and its derivative at $S_1{}^o$

We can get an intuitive interpretation by rewriting Equations (7.13) slightly:

$$\beta\left[1+G'\left(S_1+\overline{S}_2\right)\right]=1+r \qquad (7.13'a)$$

$$(1-\beta)\left[1+G'\left(\overline{S}_1+S_2\right)\right]<1+r \qquad (7.13'b)$$

The left-hand side of (7.13) shows the return each country gets for leaving one fish behind after fishing (literally, one weight unit). The fish will come back after having gained some weight (natural mortality would be accounted for in the weight gain). This is the term $1+G'(S)$, and it is multiplied by the share of the stock coming back to the country's economic zone, which can be interpreted as the probability that the country will in fact receive the gain from the investment it makes in the fish stock by leaving one more fish behind. On the right-hand side is the return on putting money in the bank. For country 1 the account balances; the expected return on leaving one more fish in the sea is exactly the same as the return on money in the bank. But for country 2 the expected return on leaving fish behind in the sea is less than the return on money in the bank, so country 2 leaves nothing behind.

The outcome could be worse. In order to have an incentive to leave anything behind, country 1 must have a large enough share of the fish stock. Suppose the maximum rate of growth of the stock is 100 per cent ($G'(0) = 1$). Suppose $r = 0.05$. For equality in Equation (7.13'a) we need $\beta \geq 0.525$, and for $r = 0.1$ we need $\beta \geq 0.55$. As more and more countries enter the fishery, the chance that we have one that is big enough gets less and less. And, if we have none that is large enough, the stock would be fished to extinction immediately.

As an aside: if the reader finds it heroic to assume that all parameters, price and interest rate in particular, remain the same for ever, then note that the conditions we have derived can also be derived from maximizing the present value over two periods. The two value functions would be

$$\text{Maximize } V_1 = p\left[\beta X_0 - S_{0,1}\right] + \frac{p}{1+r}\left\{\beta\left[S_{0,1} + \overline{S}_{0,2} + G\left(S_{0,1} + \overline{S}_{0,2}\right)\right] - S_{1,1}\right\}$$

$$\text{Maximize } V_2 = p\left[(1-\beta)X_0 - S_{0,2}\right] + \frac{p}{1+r}\left\{(1-\beta)\left[\begin{array}{c}\overline{S}_{0,1} + S_{0,2} \\ +G\left(\overline{S}_{0,1} + S_{0,2}\right)\end{array}\right] - S_{1,2}\right\}$$

$S_{0,1}$ is the stock left behind by country 1 in the first period (period 0) and $S_{1,1}$ the stock left behind in the next period, and similarly for country 2. We maximize this with respect to $S_{0,1}$ and $S_{0,2}$ only, because in the next period there is a new decision coming up with respect to how much to leave behind then ($S_{1,1}$ and $S_{1,2}$). Making the necessary calculations we would end up with Equations (7.13), and the only assumption we would have to make about price and the discount rate is that both remain the same over two periods. But, if these parameters remain the same for longer, we get, of course, a series of identical problems, just as assumed in the infinite series version of the problem.

The outcome in which country 2 leaves nothing behind is, of course, worse than if it had decided to cooperate and maximize the joint returns from the fishery. The reason country 2 takes all the fish that come its way is that leaving anything behind is just poor investment. This is the best decision country 2 can make, given what country 1 decides to leave behind and given that they do not negotiate and agree on something that would be better for both. Another way to look at the problem is to note that country 2 can take advantage of the stronger incentive country 1 has to conserve some of the stock; country 2 knows that, if country 1 has a sufficiently large share of the stock, it will conserve some of it in its own interest, and it has no way of preventing country 2 to benefit from that. This gives country 2 some of what we might call "hold-up power"; as we shall see, country 2 would in some situations not be willing to accept what might look like a fair share of the profits from a cooperative solution. It has sometimes been argued that all that countries need to do to find an acceptable sharing formula for fish catches is to calculate how many fish reside in each country's area and allocate a total catch quota accordingly. This is sometimes called the zonal attachment principle, but it is not sufficient.

To analyse this, let us define a sharing parameter for the cooperative profit. The share α goes to the dominant country and the share $1-\alpha$ to the minor country. Denote the stock level that maximizes aggregate present value by S^o, and by S^* the stock that is left behind in a competitive situation such as the one we have just analysed. If the minor player is to agree to the cooperative solution, his share of the cooperative profits (share of the total catch) will have to be at least as large as what he could get in a non-cooperative solution, which implies

$$(1-\alpha)G(S^o) \geq (1-\beta)\left[S^* + G(S^*)\right] \tag{7.14}$$

The zonal attachment principle implies that $1-\alpha = 1-\beta$. We are not guaranteed that this will work, because we could have $G(S^o) < S^* + G(S^*)$. Let us use a numerical example to illustrate this. Suppose the growth function is the logistic one used in Chapter 4, with $a = 1$ and $K = 1$. Put $r = 0.05$. In the cooperative solution, $G'(S) = a(1 - 2S) = r = 0.05$, from which we can calculate $S^o = 0.475$. S^* can be calculated from Equation (7.13'a); country 1 is the only one leaving anything behind. Equation (7.14) can then be used to calculate the critical value of $1-\alpha$. The result is shown in Figure 7.3. As we see, the minor player must in most cases be offered a larger share of the cooperative profit than that which corresponds to his share of the stock.

We can make the same kind of calculations in the case when the cost per unit of fish is sensitive to the size of the exploited stock. This would not qualitatively change our results that the zonal attachment principle does not always work and that the minor player must typically be offered a larger share of the cooperative profits than corresponds to his share of the stock. But the minor player would now leave some fish in his zone, because it would not be

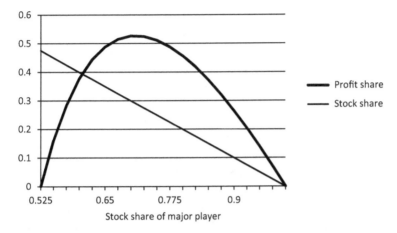

Figure 7.3 Critical share (1–α) of the cooperative profit that the minor country must be offered to be interested in a cooperative rather than a non-cooperative solution, compared with its share (1–β) of the stock

profitable to catch all of it; the cost per unit of fish caught would, ultimately, be too high. The stock would never be wiped out completely, but both countries, and especially the minor country, would leave less than the level compatible with the cooperative solution (see Hannesson 2007).

Advances in fisheries management

How successful has fisheries management been since the establishment of the 200-mile zone? Undoubtedly, a whole book could be written about it, but that is not our purpose. Here we shall note simply that progress has been made. In its latest assessment of the state of world fisheries, the FAO notes that, for assessed stocks, the average biomass has increased since early this century and was in 2016 higher than the maximum sustainable yield level. The advances in fisheries management have mainly occurred in the economically advanced countries of the world, whereas in many developing countries the status of fish stocks continues to deteriorate (FAO 2020: 55–6, box 4).

In a recent study, Christopher Costello *et al.* (2016) note that rights-based management regimes pursuing economic goals have been most successful in improving fisheries management and that their continued introduction would be the most promising avenue to further improvement. By "rights-based management" they mean management by individual transferable quotas. It is indeed likely that management by individual quotas is the key to the improvement in the status of fish stocks. Transferability is a wonderful tool to achieve economic efficiency, as will be discussed in the next chapter, but of secondary importance for the biological status of fish stocks, which depends critically on a suitable overall limit on the total catch and its effective enforcement.

We round this off with an encouraging story on international cooperation, even if it has sometimes proceeded without a formal agreement and in fact taken on the appearance of a breakdown in cooperation. In the Northeast Atlantic there are three species that migrate far and wide, as has already been mentioned: mackerel, herring and blue whiting. They pass through the exclusive economic zone of the European Union (most of this will soon end up as the zone of the United Kingdom), the Faeroe Islands, Norway, Iceland, and Greenland (mackerel). All these entities are involved in negotiating catch limits for these three species. In addition, the Northeast Atlantic Fisheries Commission is involved, as these three species pass through what is left of the high seas in the Northeast Atlantic (see Figure 6.1) and the said organization is the one with responsibility for managing fisheries in this area (recall that the UN Fish Stocks Agreement gives the responsibility for managing fisheries outside national boundaries to regional fisheries management organizations). Since these negotiations began around 1990, they have periodically failed to produce an all-inclusive agreement; there has at times been no agreement on the total amount of fish to be taken (the total quota, or total allowable catch) or on how a total quota should be shared between the countries participating in the fishery.

All three species gather in large concentrations, called schools or shoals, and they are fished mostly by encircling them by enormous bag-shaped nets (purse seines) or ensnaring them in large midwater trawls. There is some evidence that the catch per unit of effort is not sensitive to the size of the stock; as long as there are any shoals left there will be enough to fill up a boat. This means that the cost per unit of fish caught is not very sensitive to the size of the stock. For mackerel, no country has a dominant share of the stock; the pre-Brexit European Union had the largest share of the catches, which since 2010 has been around 40 per cent. For Norwegian spring-spawning herring, Norway is a dominant player, with a share of between 50 and 60 per cent. As we have seen, uncoordinated fishing is likely to result in severe decimation of stocks, and perhaps total depletion in cases such as these in which the cost per unit of fish is insensitive to the stock size and the dominant country has a share close to or below a half.

For all three stocks, annual catch quotas and their sharing are negotiated annually. It happens frequently that these negotiations do not result in a formal agreement between all the states concerned about a total catch quota and its sharing. So what has happened when the negotiations on these species have not resulted in an agreement signed by all? Figure 7.4 shows the development of the stocks of Norwegian spring-spawning herring and Northeast Atlantic mackerel since the 1980s; years without a full agreement are marked by a dotted line. We do not see any tendency for stock levels to fall in years without a formal agreement; the stocks have varied up and down as a part

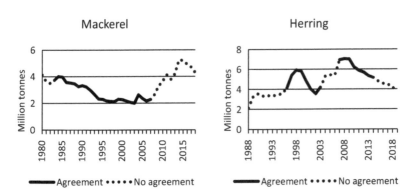

Figure 7.4 Development of the stocks of Northeast Atlantic mackerel and Norwegian spring-spawning herring, 1980–2019
Source: ICES (2019b).

of natural fluctuations. A statistical analysis of fishing mortality variations shows no tendency for it to increase in years without a formal agreement but, rather, a tendency for it to increase in years with such agreements in place (see Hannesson 2020). This indicates that the countries involved cooperate informally when they do not put any signatures on paper; they set their quotas unilaterally, and these quotas may not be to their partners' liking, but they are apparently fairly modest and nowhere near large enough to cause a precipitous fall in future catches or serious mutual retaliations. All these countries are very much aware of what happened to the Norwegian spring-spawning herring around 1970, and some of them suffered directly from that collapse. None of them seems in any mood to repeat that experience. Seen from this viewpoint, that fishery collapse was perhaps a good thing; it brought home a lesson that no one is eager to repeat.

Notes

1. For an analysis focusing on sustainable yield, but much richer and more advanced, see Pintassilgo *et al.* (2010).
2. Much of her work is listed and discussed in Frischmann, Marciano & Ramello (2019).
3. See footnote 1 in Chapter 4 and note that the profits in the first period are not discounted, so the first element in the series is x and not kx.
4. The split stream model was developed by Robert McKelvey. See, for example, Golubtsov & McKelvey (2007) and references in that paper.

8

FISHERIES MANAGEMENT

Since the 200-mile exclusive economic zone became nearly universally established in the late 1970s, fisheries management by catch quotas has become increasingly widespread. The 200-mile zone was an important precondition, because a limit on total catches from a fish stock requires control over the boats fishing that stock. When most fisheries took place outside national limits, fish quotas would have required acceptance by all nations that engaged in the fishery. If those that participated in a fishery on the high seas had agreed on a total fish quota, this could have been challenged by newcomers, who could have entered the fishery by virtue of free fishing on the high seas. Successful management by those who at one point in time participated in a fishery would have made that type of challenge all the more likely. In this chapter we shall discuss fisheries management by catch quotas, its advantages and challenges and what the main alternatives are.

Even in cases when a fish stock is entirely within the economic zone of one country, setting a total quota can be a challenge; there are often distinctly different interest groups involved, much like different countries fishing the same stock. Satisfying everyone's demands would most probably mean that the total quota would be much too high, threatening depletion of the fish stocks. Cutting through such competing claims can be difficult enough for a single government, and doing so when different countries are involved more difficult still, as the legal enforcement apparatus of the nation state cannot be relied upon; no country has jurisdiction on another's territory. The issue is even less tractable for stocks that migrate into the high seas, for reasons discussed in the previous chapter; it is more challenging to cooperate when the number of participants is large, let alone indefinite, and enforcement is more difficult on the high seas, where no country has jurisdiction except flag states over their own boats. Nevertheless, control by fish quotas has become quite widespread, even for fish stocks that are shared between a number of countries, including those that straddle into the highs seas.

The need for fish quotas, or some other instrument to limit fishing, is clear enough. In Chapter 4 we explained why uncontrolled access leads to overexploitation of fish stocks; a stock will be driven down to a lower level than it should be, because we are expending more manpower and more money on fishing than we should be, getting less in return for our efforts than we would get in other sectors of the economy. An overall fish quota does not deal with this directly, however. What it does is to limit the total catch of fish to something deemed appropriate. Further on we shall get to the economic aspects of catch quotas, but just note at this point that, if an overall catch quota is set within the limits of surplus growth, it can be supported indefinitely. Consider Figure 4.1, reproduced here as Figure 8.1. Suppose we set a catch quota $\bar{Y}$. This catch quota can be supported by two different stock levels, S_1 and S_2, ignoring natural fluctuations, as $\bar{Y} = G(S_1) = G(S_2)$. More generally, by setting a total catch quota within the limits set by the surplus growth, we can make sure that the fishery is sustainable.

Note that, if the actual stock level is different from either S_1 or S_2 when we set the catch quota $\bar{Y}$, the stock will automatically approach the level supporting the set catch quota if the stock is larger than S_1. The arrows in Figure 8.1 show how the stock changes if the catch is different from surplus growth ($Y \neq G$). If $S < S_1$, the stock will decline towards zero unless the catch quota is reduced sufficiently to rebuild the stock to S_1, which would support the catch quota $\bar{Y}$. This alerts us to the fact that catch quotas must be set with reference to the actual stock size; if the stock needs to be rebuilt, the quota must be less than the surplus growth to allow the necessary rebuilding to take place.

Individual quotas

Economically, little will be achieved by an overall catch quota alone. The overall quota might suffice to avoid driving the stock to extinction, given that it is kept within the limits set by the surplus growth. That is, of course,

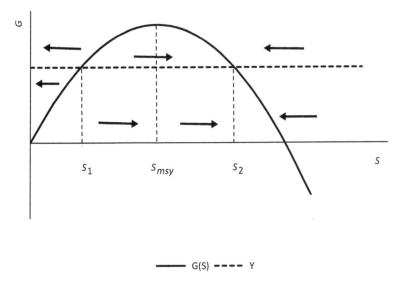

— G(S) ---- Y

Figure 8.1 How the stock changes if the catch (Y) is different from surplus growth (G)

an accomplishment; the world has seen fish stocks crash because of overexploitation. But an overall quota must be enforced somehow. One possibility is to stop the fishery just in time when the overall quota limit has been reached. This has been tried, with predictable results, which are economically disastrous. Knowing that the fishery will be stopped at some point, the fishermen will compete as much as they can to catch as many fish as possible before the overall limit has been reached. This leads to a compressed fishing season, lower-quality product than need be and ghost fishing by fishing gear lost or abandoned in the water in the race for the fish. This approach was tried for years in the Alaskan halibut fishery. At its worst, the fishery was down to two 24-hour "openings", and most of the fish was frozen. After individual quotas were put in place, the fishery was spread over eight months of the year and most of the product went to the much better-paying fresh fish market.

The competition for a limited overall quota thus leads to economic waste of its own kind. In Chapter 4 we showed how open access to a fish stock leads to excessive fishing effort, which means overinvestment in fishing boats and excessive use of manpower. With free access to a given overall fish quota there will be competition for the largest possible share. People will invest in boats and other equipment to get the fish as quickly as possible, as long as they get a better return in the fishery than they could get elsewhere. This will typically lead to a larger fishing fleet than necessary, and the result is a shrinking fishing season with all its consequences: a poor-quality product, ghost fishing by lost gear and even loss of life and limb if fishermen get too eager and the openings happen in a period with bad weather. All these problems were well known in the Alaskan halibut fishery.[1]

The solution to this is to divide the overall fish quota into individual units – that is, individual quotas. This is what has happened sooner or later in fisheries that have become quota-controlled, because of the race for fish that otherwise is prone to develop. Needless to say, allocating quotas to individual fishermen or firms has often been problematic. There are few if any objective criteria for allocating individual quotas that are unassailable and everyone will immediately accept. One criterion that seems to have much to recommend itself is fishing history. Fishermen have been offered individual quotas equal to the share of the total catch they took over some period in the past – three years, for example. This would seem fair, especially when the situation is such that the total fish catch must be reduced because of previous overexploitation together with worsening environmental conditions. The total catch will then have to be reduced, and with a share of the total similar to what it was in the past the good fishermen would be guaranteed to continue to do well, in relative terms, and the less clever or lucky ones not worse than they used to, again in relative terms. Sometimes investment in fishing boats has been included as an additional criterion, as newcomers may have committed a lot of money but not yet accumulated much fishing experience.

Another possibility is to allocate individual quotas with reference to the kind of boat that is being used. Individual boat quotas in the Norwegian fisheries were originally determined on the basis of the size of the boats, either in terms of length (the cod fishery) or volume (hectolitres of cargo capacity in the pelagic fisheries). This, needless to say, disadvantages those who for some reason or other are able to take larger catches with equipment similar to that of others. It can be debated which method is fairer: catch history or the characteristics of the boats used.

Often, and perhaps even as a rule, individual fish quotas have been imposed when a "crisis" has developed. This was the case in the Alaskan halibut fishery, in which the shortness of the fishing season had become bothersome to the point of absurdity. It was the case in Norway, where the catches from the Northeast Arctic cod had declined severely and both the Norwegian and the Soviet authorities recognized the need to limit the total catch and rebuild the stock. The Norwegian coastal fleet had for years been exempt from quota regulations, resulting in more Norwegian fishing than was intended, and in 1990 the Norwegian coastal fleet was put under a regime of individual quotas. This was originally meant to be a temporary remedy, but the quota arrangement had come to stay. Similarly, in Iceland, a crisis in the herring fishery in the 1970s made it necessary to severely restrict the amount of fish caught by each boat, resulting in individual boat quotas. These quotas turned out to be ridiculously small, so, rather than rig up all the necessary outfit, some were happy to let others take their quota. Thus began the transferability of quotas in the Icelandic fisheries, by default, as it were.[2] A few years later, in the early 1980s, a crisis developed in the Icelandic cod fisheries. The Icelanders had chased the foreign fleets away when they established their exclusive economic zone, but the Icelandic fleet expanded quickly while the cod stock declined, and it became necessary to limit the catches severely. The method chosen was individual boat quotas, whereby boats were given a share in the overall quota on the basis of their catch history. It bears noting that this arrangement was initiated by the industry "parliament", a meeting at which the entire industry was represented, and the national parliament later affirmed its support by the necessary legislation. Also in Iceland, the prevailing notion was that this was an emergency measure that would soon be reversed, but the need to control fish catches by quotas or some other method did not go away; it became even more accentuated.

Sometimes governments and legislatures take a more hands-on approach. This was the case in the Alaska pollock fishery, which is the largest fishery in the United States and one of the largest in the world. As we have already mentioned, this fishery was Americanized in 1976 when the US government established a fishery protection zone, later renamed exclusive economic zone in accordance with the Convention on the Law of the Sea. The market for Alaska pollock developed rapidly, and investments in boats and processing facilities ballooned. The fishing capacity of the fleet soon exceeded the productivity of the stock and an overall catch limit was put in place, for which the boats could compete. The results were predictable: shorter and shorter fishing seasons and overcapacity in the processing industry, with an emphasis on products that could be processed quickly (surimi instead of fillets). Attempts to get the industry to agree on individual quotas failed. In 1998 the US Congress cut the Gordian knot by passing the American Fisheries Act, which explicitly named which boats could or could not participate in the fishery. This eliminated the overcapacity of the fleet and was the beginning of the individual quota system in the Alaska pollock fishery, now known as the quota share system. This was all the more remarkable as there was at the time a moratorium on setting up new individual transferable quota systems, such as had been in place in some American fisheries for years; during this moratorium the pros and cons of such systems were studied, under the auspices of the National Research Council.[3] The lawmakers got around this by enabling fisheries cooperatives to be formed. These cooperatives got fish quota allocations, and the fishing companies were permitted to join fishing cooperatives, which then allocated quotas to the boats. The results were predictable: longer fishing seasons and more emphasis on products of higher quality (fillets) that took longer to produce.

Transferability of quotas

Transferability of individual quotas is a very important policy tool, controversial though it is. Transferability has different aspects. One is leasing versus selling. If somebody leases his quota he retains the ownership, but somebody else can catch the fish that the quota allows him to take. There are several things to be said in support of this kind of arrangement. One is flexibility. Somebody may have a boat that is too small to allow effective utilization of the quota the owner has, and there might be others who could put an additional quota to good use. In a situation such as that, both parties and the industry as a whole would gain from allowing one to lease some or all of his quota to another. More generally, boatowners may have different fishing costs, and those with low costs could utilize the quotas of others more efficiently. When a stock is in a poor shape because of poor recruitment or whatever, the total quota will be small. It could then make sense for some quota owners to lease their quota to someone else rather than rig their boats for a short and unprofitable fishing season. There are many circumstances in which it would make sense for someone to lease his quota temporarily and for others to lease it in temporarily. Allowing leasing would result in catching the fish in the cheapest possible way, which is a gain for all, and for society as a whole as well.

Nevertheless, leasing is often restricted, or even outright forbidden. For some, the reason seems to be aversion to people earning money for something other than the sweat of their brow. If this idea were applied with full force throughout society, the results could be wide-ranging and possibly quite bad: what if it is forbidden to earn money from real estate, from owning bonds or stocks, or from whatever asset one might hold? What typically causes outrage in the fisheries setting is that somebody might have got a fish quota for free, on the basis of catch history or whatever, and then decided to stop fishing and use their quota as a retirement fund, renting it out to others. Those other, active, fishermen would be paying for the privilege to get access to the fish, which originally was a common resource and free for all. The rapid progress of fishing technology has in many, and perhaps most, cases made it impossible to keep that arrangement: everybody can have something when there is more than enough for all, but when there is not enough for all it must be rationed somehow. This has happened in one fishery after another and has often been resolved by individual catch quotas. What has accentuated this problem is that access to a fish stock has often become very valuable very quickly, and those who got their quotas for free, sometimes in dire straits when the industry was virtually bankrupt, all of a sudden found themselves in possession of a valuable asset. All at once they found themselves with something that they had got for free, almost as poverty relief, that they could now rent out or sell for a substantial sum. It is, up to a point, possible to understand those who can no longer do as previous generations did and start fishing with little capital other than a boat, having now to purchase not just a boat but also the fish quota that is the precondition for using it. In principle this is not different, however, from having to buy or rent a farm, or a shop or an office in a good location.

Economists are fond of pointing out that the solution to this is access fees. Instead of renting or buying fish quotas from private individuals or firms, one would get it from the government in exchange for paying an access fee, perhaps through an auction of quotas, as some economists have recommended. It can be argued that the government would be a more legitimate recipient of these access fees than ex-fishermen rentiers, but access must be limited in any event if the fish stocks and the efficiency of the industry are to be maintained. It is often regretted that those who later turn out to be the owners of valuable fish quotas did not have to pay for them when they were originally allocated, but then we forget the history of how these fish quotas often came into being in the first place. As already stated, they have often been an emergency solution to a crisis in the industry, which was not even breaking even economically at the time the quotas were introduced. Selling quotas to fishermen or firms under those circumstances would have been a forlorn hope. Suppose somebody in the industry had predicted – correctly, as it turned out – that the fish quotas would become very profitable in a certain number of years. Penniless as they would probably have been, they would have had to persuade the bankers to lend them money because this would be a good investment. Would they have believed them? Giving quotas for free to an industry in crisis was, in many situations, the only way to go. Some people might have correctly expected that these quotas would gain value over time. This may have contributed to the quota solution being acceptable in the first place; it has often been touch and go in the industry about these things, and some might have seen the possibility of getting a windfall gain from a fish quota given out for free and found the quota solution acceptable for that reason. Simplifying a little, it is the first generation of quota owners that gets the windfall gain; the second generation must pay its way in, but may expect to get its money back when leaving the industry. So the windfall gain is a once-and-for-all thing, and can be regarded as a necessary cost to implement an effective fisheries management system.

It is important to emphasize that the quota value is not something that is taken from anyone, but is generated by a better management system. To see where the value of a fish quota comes from, consider Figure 4.3 in Chapter 4, reproduced here with a slight modification as Figure 8.2. The effort under open access will be E^*; at this point the average productivity (AP), the value of the catch per unit of effort, is equal to the cost per unit of effort, as explained in Chapter 4. The optimal level of effort is E^o, when the marginal productivity (MP) is equal to the cost per unit of effort; at this point the marginal unit of effort – or the last boat, as it may be put – is contributing a value to the fishery exactly equal to what it costs. At this optimal point, the difference between the total revenue and the total cost is maximal; this is the fishery rent that reflects the scarcity value of the fish stock. This is what those who participate in the fishery would be willing to pay for the privilege of having access to the fish stock. The value of this annual rent, capitalized as present value over the time horizon the fish quotas are valid (which could be indefinite), is the value of the total quota in the fishery if it is set at the level implying optimal effort. The fishing rent is generated by reducing fishing effort and building up the fish stock to a level with a higher productivity.

The advantage of individual transferable quotas is that they initiate a development that moves the fishery away from the open-access situation to optimal fishing. As already stated, quotas have usually been put in place when the fishery is in crisis. The open-access situation can hardly be called a crisis – the industry is just breaking even – but let us then keep in mind that deterministic models such as this one are not a good representation under all circumstances; when fish stocks are down because of adverse environ-mental conditions, we can expect the situation to be a lot worse than it is on average under open access. Putting individual quotas in place and making them transferable provides an opportunity for those with lower fishing costs to buy quotas from others with higher costs at a price advantageous to both. This initiates a process of rationalization by which more efficient fishermen or fishing firms buy out less efficient ones. The alert reader will note that in Figure 8.2 all have the same cost, but this is of course a simplification. In reality some fishermen have lower cost than others, and under open access it is the one with the highest cost who breaks even, while others make some profit over and above what they need to pay for their capital. Despite this cost difference, open access will still result in excessive fishing effort, so the simple model of Figure 4.3 and 8.2 is sufficient to explain that result.

Over time, full transferability of quotas tends to lead to a maximally effi-cient industry, yielding a maximum resource rent. How can that come about? Suppose an industry is controlled by an overall quota. This overall quota is perfectly divisible and saleable. Suppose somebody wants to buy a new boat. It could be someone who owns a boat from before and needs a renewal or it could be someone who has never been in the industry before. To be able to operate a boat, a quota of an appropriate size is needed. Someone who has a boat from before, but finds out that a bigger boat is more economical, must buy an additional quota, and someone who begins from scratch must buy a quota from scratch. If there are enough who are ready to sell their quota, the

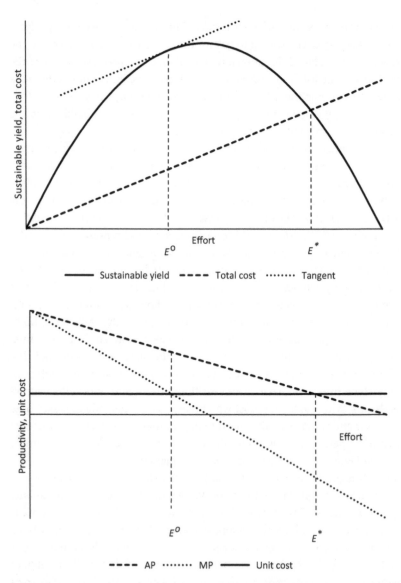

Figure 8.2 Open-access effort (E*) versus optimal effort (E°) and the value of a fish quota (difference between cost line and the sustainable yield curve) under optimal fishing

investment in the new boat will take place, with an old boat, or perhaps more than one, being taken out of the fishing fleet. If there are insufficient sellers of quotas, then no new boat is needed. The point is that the fishing fleet will be renewed at the pace that is necessary. "Excessive" capitalization is often seen as a major problem in the fishery, and this is in fact what occurs in the open-access fishery, as we have seen, but this is not a problem in a fishery controlled by individual transferable quotas. If somebody wants to buy a bigger and more expensive boat than they need, well, then, that is their problem. If the quota control is effective, the fish stock will not be fished excessively, and, if someone wants to fish their quota at a higher cost than needed, that would be worst for them.

The capitalization of resource rent into quota values poses a problem for estimating the benefits from quota-controlled fisheries. Those who think these benefits will be reflected in higher profits of fishing companies as they appear on their books will not find what they are looking for. For those who have bought quotas to facilitate their fishing operations, the quota value is a cost, just like the purchase of a fishing boat, and interest on loans taken to acquire such quotas will be a financial cost, just as is interest on loans taken to purchase a boat. In economic terms, purchases of quotas are not a cost but a transfer; the value of a quota represents a gain in efficiency, not a real cost necessary to produce fish. Therefore, the profits of fishing companies provide few or no clues to what a quota management system may have accomplished. In equilibrium, the return on capital will be the same across all industries, adjusted eventually for different levels of risk. Hence, the return on capital in a quota-managed industry will be the same as in an open-access industry, the difference being that in the quota-managed industry there will be an additional category of capital – that is, the quota value that represents the scarcity value of the underlying fish stock.[4] Therefore, studies using companies' accounts typically find a much lower resource rent than bioeconomic studies of fisheries (Byrne, Agnarsson & Davidsdóttir 2019).

Control of quotas

A major problem with fisheries management by individual fish quotas is the need for control. Fisheries management by fish quotas is an invitation to cheat. Any fish that is not declared under the quota regime is a licence to take another fish legally. In multi-species fisheries in which different types of fish fetch different prices there will be an incentive to declare large catches of cheap fish when most of the catch consists of more valuable fish. And fish of the same species are not necessarily all equal; small cod often are less valuable than larger ones. In our discussion of the Northern cod of Newfoundland, we mentioned that a contributing factor in the collapse was that fishermen threw small cod overboard in order not to use up their valuable quotas.

The efficiency of a fish quota regime therefore depends critically on the ability to monitor what is going on and adequately punish those who do not follow the rules. Ideally, this monitoring needs to take place both in the boats when at sea and on shore when the fish are landed. Monitoring at sea is necessary because of the incentives fishermen have to throw away less valuable fish. Many countries have mandatory observers on board fishing boats to avoid discards of fish. Onboard cameras could conceivably help as well. It is difficult to know how serious this problem is, but there are certain obvious limits; no fisherman has ever got rich from throwing away fish at sea.

Monitoring onshore is easier. Fish usually go through several points in the chain from the wharf to the dinner table, and by checking reports at one point against reports at another it is possible to check whether the monitoring is effective. Countries such as New Zealand, Norway and Iceland that practise quota management have set up elaborate schemes of this kind, requiring all fish to be weighed at officially approved weighing stations and then checking as they pass through various points from landing to processing to export. Even so, every now and then there pops up some scandal involving quota busting. Monitoring quota regimes is not cheap, and fisheries in the United States and Canada that have been put under a quota regime have to pay a fee on fish landings to cover these monitoring costs. These costs have to be put against the gains from a quota management system.

There are undoubtedly many circumstances when a quota management regime cannot be expected to work. Small-scale fisheries conducted with small boats catching a multitude of fish species and landing their catches in highly informal circumstances on the beach would not be good candidates for a quota management system. The integrity of the civil service in a country is also an important factor; if the fish are valuable and the landings inspector is poorly paid, they can probably be persuaded to look the other way if something "fishy" is going on.

Alternatives to quota management

In cases when fish quotas are difficult to implement, what can be done instead? Effort controls have a longer pedigree than quota controls. Effort controls could be characterized as going to the root of the problem. In Chapter 4 we saw how open access leads to too much effort, depleting fish stocks, and too much investment in fishing boats and excessive use of manpower. Effort controls address this problem directly.

We can distinguish between short- and long-term effort controls. Short-term effort controls are put in place when the capacity of the fishing fleet threatens the immediate viability of fish stocks. In previous chapters we have discussed how fish stocks fluctuate over time. When a stock is in a poor shape, caused by adverse environmental conditions and perhaps aggravated by overfishing, it will probably be necessary to force the fishing fleet to take a smaller quantity of fish out of the sea than it is able to. That is what happened with the Norwegian spring-spawning herring in the late 1960s. One way of dealing with this is to apply fish quotas, but we are looking at cases when that is not a preferred method, for whatever reason. The alternative is to force the fishing fleet to be idle some of the time it could be fishing. A limited number of fishing days is how this is typically implemented. Fishermen are permitted to go fishing only two days a week, or three, or just one – whatever is deemed within the limits the fish stock can withstand. Limits can also be set to how much fish by weight they are allowed to bring ashore (trip limits), but then we are moving towards control by quotas.

Fishing days are certainly easier to monitor and enforce than a quota control system. Fishing boats can be seen and counted easily, and even at sea their activities can be monitored through devices that send signals to a monitoring station, recording their position at regular intervals and providing information about speed, from which may be inferred whether or not the boat is fishing. Even so, this method has its own problems. Fishermen can load on more gear than usual and thereby increase the fishing power of their boats. Fishing days have been widely used as a regulatory method, but they do little or nothing to address the main problem, which is the incentive to overinvest in fishing boats. It is true that, if boats cannot be used all the time they could be used, the returns on investing in a boat will be less and the incentive to invest weaker, but if fishing days regulations need to be in place it is a sure sign that there is overcapacity in the industry, so limiting fishing days cannot be a long-term solution to the problem of overinvestment.

Fishing licences constitute a type of effort control that deals with the incentive to overinvest. This would seem to go straight to the heart of the problem, which is that in an open-access fishery there will be too many boats. It needs to be assessed how many boats are needed in the fishery, and then licences can be issued for the boats needed. But boats come in all shapes and sizes. If a fishing licence does not specify further what the boats should be like, the licence holder may invest in a large and technically efficient boat to get as much fishing power as possible from its licence. Fishing licences therefore need to be specific as to what kind of boat the licence holder is allowed to operate. This has led to self-defeating regulations about the size and design of boats. Fishing effort is a multidimensional variable; there are many factors that affect the technical capacity of fishing boats. There have been, and still are, regulations in place about the length of boats; a licence may stipulate how long the boat is that the license holder may operate. But boat designers are very clever in circumventing such regulations; they design boats that are almost as wide as they are long and have much greater fishing power than a boat of that length used to have. And then there is the possibility of fitting out a boat with better equipment – fish finders, winches, better gear, whatever – that enhances the fishing power of a boat of a given length or tonnage. Technological progress ensures that the number of boats that at one time may have been adequate to fish a stock optimally will at a later time be much too large. An industry person, a fan of technologically advanced fishing, once characterized the traditional hand line as a piece of string with a hook on one end and an idiot on the other. This may have been true at one point, but not so certainly any more. The modern "hand line" is a machine with many hooks on one end and a computer-controlled winch at the other, which jigs the line and pulls it up automatically when enough fish have been trapped on the hooks in the water. A small one-man boat with several such machines has a fishing power of a boat many times its size decades ago and with a sizable crew.

These points alert us to one advantage of individual transferable quotas: they accommodate technological progress much better than effort controls. In a quota management system, boatowners have an incentive to tailor their investments in boats and equipment to the quota they have; it makes no sense to buy a bigger boat or better equipment than they need to fish the quota they have at the lowest possible cost. And, if new boats or better equipment might pay off better with a larger quota holding, it would make sense to buy an additional quota to make a larger-scale operation possible. A fishery scientist once characterized effort controls as a desperate race between controls and technology; technical progress made the boats ever more efficient, so the effort controls had to be tightened continuously. This problem does not arise under quota controls.

Quotas for fluctuating fish stocks

How well do quota controls cope with fluctuations in fish stocks? As we have seen, they can be substantial and sudden. Quotas must be set with due regard to the abundance of the fish stocks and in a timely fashion. A quota control could be disastrous if fisheries scientists overestimate the abundance of fish; the stock could be wiped out before anyone realized what was happening.

This argues for using quota controls for stocks that vary moderately over time and such that errors at one point can be corrected in a timely fashion later. Nevertheless, quota controls could be even more necessary for stocks that vary substantially on a short timescale. One such is the capelin in the Barents Sea, which we discussed in Chapter 5. There is now a long track record of quota control in this fishery, and often it has been shut down completely. There is also a long track record of quota controls for other fluctuating stocks, in Europe, North America and elsewhere. There is no case of quota control having led to depletion of stocks, except in Newfoundland, where the fishery for the Northern cod was cut back too late, probably for avoiding unemployment in the industry rather than mistaken science. It needs to be emphasized that quota control must be based on a timely and reasonably accurate fish stock assessment, but, despite its shortcomings, fishery science seems to have come a long way in this regard; there are no cases known to this author of fish stocks having been endangered because of a mistaken quota setting.

One question to be asked in this context is whether fish quotas should be set with a view to stabilize fish catches from fluctuating stocks. There are economic reasons for preferring stable catches to fluctuating ones: they provide a more even utilization of capacity in the processing industry and a more even flow of products to the consumer market. But such stabilization could be risky; the industry would be catching a larger share of a small stock than of a big stock. Taking a stable catch from a fluctuating stock would probably mean catching a lot fewer fish than one would do on average if the quota were set as a fraction of a fluctuating stock. For stocks that fluctuate enormously, such as the Barents Sea capelin or the California sardine, stabilization of catches would not be possible.

One country, New Zealand, has experimented with endowing its fishing industry with fixed annual quotas of a newly discovered fish species, the orange roughy, discussed in Chapter 2. The idea was that the government would buy back quotas from industry when there was a need to limit the catch in years when the stock was down, and sell additional quotas to the industry when the stock was in better condition. This turned out to be financially disastrous and was abandoned. Not much was known about the orange roughy at the time. This is a fish that grows slowly and has a very long lifespan (decades), and the stock turned out to be much less productive than initially thought.

Most quota-setting rules aim at catching a certain fraction of the stock. We have discussed two such cases: the Northeast Arctic cod and the Norwegian spring-spawning herring. The rule for the cod is slightly modified depending on the size of the spawning stock; the other one is based on a target fishing mortality. This means that the annual fish quota will go up and down together with the stock. So will the individual quotas, which are determined as shares of the total quota. The individual quotas for these species in Norway are transferable with certain restrictions, so what boatowners are buying or selling are shares in future annual total quotas that will go up and down depending on the status of the stocks. To get back to our previous discussion about investment incentives, those who buy quotas to ensure they have a sufficient base to operate a boat would have to guess how large fish catches their quota share allocations will give them in the future. Past experience will provide a clue, and the expertise of fisheries scientists can also be consulted.

Effort controls are often supposed to deal much better with fluctuations in fish stocks than quota controls do. This is based on the production function we discussed in Chapter 4 (Equation 4.3), which was

$$Y = qES$$

where Y is the catch of fish, E is fishing effort and S is the stock. With this specification, the catch of fish will vary directly with the stock, for any given level of effort. To put it differently, if we fix the effort, we will always catch a certain fraction of the stock. But reality is considerably more complicated than this abstraction. We have already discussed the problems of measuring, or even defining, fishing effort, something we need to do if the effort is to be kept at some given level. And then there are the conditions that must hold if this production function is to be valid; the fish stock is always evenly distributed in the sea over a given area, so that its density is directly proportional to its size. As we have discussed, for stocks that migrate in shoals, this assumption is likely not to be satisfied. The catch per unit of effort may hold up well almost to the end; as it was once put, the last shoal of fish could be enough to fill up your boat. But these are the types of fish that tend to vary most dramatically and for which tight controls must be applied in adverse circumstances. Quota controls are therefore likely to be most pressing for these types of fish, even if it is more difficult to assess their abundance than for species that vary more moderately. In fact, quota controls are widely applied for such fish, such as herring, capelin and mackerel.

Landing fees as a control mechanism

There has been considerable debate, both among the public and in economics journals, about landing fees as control instruments (see Weitzman 2002). In theory, landing fees could replace other instruments such as catch quotas or effort controls. How they would work we can see from a figure such as 4.3 in Chapter 4, reproduced here as Figure 8.3 with some changes. An addition is the average productivity, evaluated by price less the landings tax, formally

$$AP_{tax} = \frac{(p-t)Y}{E}$$

AP_{tax} is the value of the catch per unit of effort, evaluated at the price the fisherman gets – that is, price after tax $(p - t)$. As explained in Chapter 4, in an open-access fishery the effort would tend towards the point where the average product is equal to the cost per unit of effort. As Figure 8.3 shows, by a suitable landings tax the average productivity can be made to cross the cost line at the same point as the marginal productivity line without tax, and the economic equilibrium under open access would coincide with the economic optimum.

In the long term this would work; perhaps not as well as this simplified, deterministic model shows, but a tax on landings would definitely reduce the profitability of the fishery and thereby the incentive to invest. But, as a tool to control a fishery in the short term, this approach would be woefully inadequate. The catches from a fish stock that is in poor condition need to be curtailed in a timely fashion. How would a landings fee work? It would reduce the profitability of landings, and the landings fee is supposed to do this so that each fisherman or fishing firm stops fishing when the value of a kilogram of fish has fallen to a level equal to the cost per kilogram of fish. This would need to happen when the actual catch has reached a level equal to the permissible

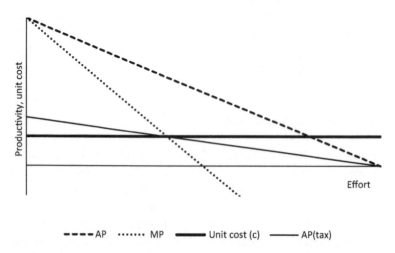

Figure 8.3 How a tax on landings generates optimal effort by having average productivity after tax intersect the unit cost of effort where marginal productivity is equal to the unit cost of effort (c)

catch, given the condition of the stock. But the fisheries managers are unlikely to know the cost per kilogram of fish for all those who they are trying to regulate. It also has to be taken into account that the relevant costs are variable costs – those associated with a fishing trip. Fixed costs are irrelevant; the idea is to discourage an additional fishing trip when the total allowable catch has been taken. Finally, even if the authorities know something about the cost of fishing, they need not know much about how it varies with the stock. The idea behind fishery control by landing fees is that fishermen would stop fishing when the stock has fallen to a level where the cost per kilogram of fish is equal to the price per kilogram less the landings fee. As discussed in Chapter 4, for some stocks the cost per unit of fish landed need not be very sensitive to the exploited stock, and, if it is not, the landings fee will fail.

One reason the landings fee has been touted by some economists is that they think that the quota values that have accrued to those who initially got them for free are ill-gotten gains. It is well known that taxes on rents are the best of all taxes; they do not lead to the distortions that accompany other taxes, such as an income tax. A tax on capital income weakens the incentive to save and invest, a tax on wages and salaries reduces the incentive to work. A tax on factors given by nature such as land, fish in the sea or oil and minerals, creams off some of the surplus income (rent) associated with exploiting these resources and can in principle be designed in such a way that it does not weaken the incentives to do so. This is a problem unrelated to controlling fishing effort or fish catches. If the rents in the fishery, as they become capitalized in the value of fish quotas, are considered ill-gotten gains, there are ways to deal with that. Quota holdings can be taxed and so can their utilization, not for the purpose of controlling the industry but for capturing some of the resource rent. Society can be considered as the ultimate owner of fish resources within the exclusive economic zone, and the industry would be paying for the privilege of utilizing them for its own benefit. Natural resource industries such as mining and, particularly, oil and gas extraction are usually taxed, and sometimes heavily, on the basis of this philosophy. That method could also be applied to the fishing industry. Governments do this in some cases. In Iceland there is a resource rent tax levied on the fishing industry, which for decades has been managed by individual transferable quotas. The government of the Falkland Islands gets a substantial part of its income from taxing or leasing its fish resources to the industry. But it is hardly a coincidence that we find this arrangement in small countries that are relatively rich in fish resources. In most countries, fishing is not a major activity, and neither is it particularly profitable.

The opinion that income due to the productivity of nature should be taxed has long been held by many economists. Income of this kind is not a remuneration for entrepreneurship, for saving or for work effort; it is a windfall gain due to owning a productive piece of land, or a building site in a good location, or rich oilfields or mines. All these we can regard as gifts of nature and not the result of any human productive effort. There are plenty of examples of owners of such natural endowments living from the rents the ownership provides and letting others do the work. The single tax movement, which once was strong in the United States, built on this sentiment; the followers of this movement thought that government expenses in the United States could be financed by a tax on land alone.[5] With regard to fishing rents, we should perhaps ask the question if governments would necessarily spend this money more wisely than the owners of the fish quotas, the value of which is capitalized resource rents. As to the fairness, these quota owners are often individuals who at an earlier stage in life got dirt under their nails.

The political economy of fisheries

When circumstances allow fisheries to be managed by individual transferable quotas, this is in many ways an ideal system. Governments undertake the role of guarding the fish stocks. They hire fisheries scientists to monitor the stocks and provide the factual basis for setting catch quotas, and they set up agencies to monitor fish catches and landings to make sure that the quotas are not overfished. This is all governments need to do, and there are people who think this could be taken care of by industry organizations in the industry's self-interest. The decisions as to who should catch the fish and how, where, when and with what type of equipment can be left to the industry itself. Given tightly enough monitored fish quotas, the individuals and firms making up the industry have an incentive to catch the fish they are entitled to in a way that minimizes costs and maximizes the value of fish pulled out of the sea.

Such minimalist government involvement in fisheries would be hard to find. Governments, even those that apply individual transferable quotas, are deeply involved in how the fish are caught and who gets to do it. The reason, basically, is akin to the "china shop principle": you break it, you own it. Once governments have taken on the role of managing fisheries, they set themselves up as the arbiter of how fishing should be done, by whom and, not least, how much should be caught. Since what governments do is the outcome of politics, what they do is open to attempts at persuasion by a public that has goals beyond or perhaps contradictory to outcomes produced by markets, cost minimization and the sustainable management of fish stocks.

We can distinguish two arenas in which fisheries policy beyond fisheries management for material benefit plays out: (a) environmental issues and (b) allocation or access issues.

Consider, first, the environmental issues. We have touched upon these already. Small, pelagic fish such as sardine and anchovy constitute food for seabirds and marine mammals. There is a segment of public opinion that thinks that the needs of these animals should be considered when setting catch quotas for sardines and anchovies, and other types of fish as well. It is undoubtedly difficult to assess what these needs are, but there is no doubt that this would involve trading off demand for feeding humans against feeding animals in the wild. Even if the sardines and the anchovies are not consumed by people directly but go into fishmeal, they ultimately end up as food for humans after passing through the stomachs of salmon or pigs and poultry.

Another environmental issue is incidental catches of birds or other animals by some types of fishing gear. There is concern that long line fishing in the Southern Ocean harms certain birds such as petrels and albatrosses. There is an international agreement on albatrosses and petrels from 2001 that has been signed by 13 nations.[6] The Southern Indian Ocean Fisheries Agreement has provisions about fishing gear design and lighting on board boats to minimize the incidental catches of seabirds. Tuna fishing in the eastern Pacific has long been under pressure to minimize incidental catches of dolphins and turtles. Fisheries managers in California are under pressure to ban all targeted catching of the California sardine, as it is an important forage fish for other marine life. It is unlikely that a fishmeal industry in

California based on the sardine could develop again, even if the abundance of the sardine rose to its previous heights.

The pressure on fisheries management authorities is probably greatest, however, from the industry itself. The industry has much influence on the management authorities, and this is often formalized as management committees made up of industry people and public administrators. The industry is often far from able to speak with one voice, though. The industry is segmented; there are owners of large trawlers or purse seiners down to small boats and they typically have very different opinions about how catch quotas should be allocated, and some are not at all happy with having it done through a market in which quotas go to the highest bidder. Small-scale fishermen have the advantage of numbers; they vote in elections, and political parties are therefore likely to pander to them, even if the bulk of fish catches is taken by large boats, sometimes owned by multi-vessel vertically integrated companies. Small-scale fishermen are influential in Iceland and Norway and many other countries and often perceive themselves in antagonistic terms to the rest of the industry, especially the trawler fleet. In Iceland this lobby group emerged almost overnight; when the quota system for cod was first put into effect in 1984, boats under 10 tonnes took only 3 per cent of the cod catch. Why bother about such a marginal group? The next year 800 small boats were purchased, and by the mid-1990s the cod catches of small boats surpassed 20 per cent of the cod catches. In the meantime, a vocal pressure group of small boat operators had emerged, and there was a constant political struggle as to whether and how to include them in the quota management system. As of 2020 this group has its own particular quota regime set aside for itself.

What makes small boat operators a thorny issue is that a dividing line between small-scale commercial operators and recreational fishing is often blurred. Fish resources used to be common resources that people exploited for their own livelihood. Why should it not be a self-evident right that they could also use this common resource for recreational purposes? This issue arises in many countries, New Zealand being one of them, but that country was one of the pioneers of a quota management system that has now been in use since 1984, and even longer for the orange roughy fishery.

In Norway, quotas in the groundfish fisheries (cod and similar species) are first allocated between different boat groups and then to individual boats. There is an allocation between the trawlers and the smaller boats, and for the latter there is an allocation between boats of different length groups, before the allocation between the individual boats. The rationale of this system is best illustrated by the fact that, if somebody buys a new and larger boat, they remain in the same boat group as before. A distinction is made between the actual length and the official length of the boat.

Quota regimes worldwide

Since the establishment of the 200-mile limit, quota-based management has become increasingly widespread. The pioneers were New Zealand and Iceland. The latter has already been mentioned. In New Zealand the quota management began in the orange roughy fishery in the early 1980s, which had been recently developed and was conducted by a few large trawlers, some of which were chartered from other countries. A few years later the quota management system was implemented in all fisheries in New Zealand, and it has remained in place since then.[7]

In both Iceland and New Zealand there are few restrictions on the transferability of quotas, and in Iceland in particular this has led to considerable structural change in the industry: fewer boats and larger firms, as well as a certain geographical concentration. Usually, however, there are restrictions on transferability that are meant to slow down or prohibit structural changes. Fisheries management is government policy, and policy is the outcome of various kinds of political pressures applied to government officials and policy makers. Even if transferable quotas promote efficiency overall, some players in the industry could be adversely affected, or perceive themselves to be adversely affected. They will, of course, try to influence the political process to further their interests as best they can. Then there are those with an ideological agenda, disliking market-based processes for whatever reason, perhaps because they reward the successful and increase income differences. But this is how the market economy works, and the historical evidence is rather negative about alternative ways to organize the economy. Furthermore, the fishing industry is hardly the most glaring example of these consequences.

Then there are objectives other than food production that may be judged important for fisheries policy. Ecological considerations for marine life have been mentioned, and so have recreational fisheries, where food production may be a minor consideration and perhaps purely coincidental.

All these diverse interests will try to influence fisheries management, and the outcome is going to be whatever politicians believe best serves their interests. All the compromises that need to be done in policy making will influence the final design of a quota management system or whatever other system is chosen. For the quota management system this will mean various restrictions on transferability, the division of quotas between different vessel groups, and much else. Therefore, quota management systems across the world vary widely in their design; some are little more than individual vessel quotas with little or no transferability and industry structure frozen fast in time, but, at their minimum, such systems avoid a destructive race for the fish and a further aggravation of the overcapacity in the industry.

The first fisheries in the United States managed by individual transferable quotas were the surf clams and ocean quahog fisheries off the mid-Atlantic states, put under quota management in 1990. The website of NOAA lists 17 fisheries in the United States as being under what they call "a quota share system", which means individual transferable quotas.[8] These fisheries have individual quota management in common, but all have different rules about transferability that were put in place by the political process by which these programmes were designed. This process is played out mainly through the regional fisheries management councils, which are responsible for formulating fisheries management measures and where industry is represented. There are eight of these in the United States.

In Canada several fisheries are under individual quota management, one of them being the Pacific halibut, a fish stock shared with the United States. The Canadian quota management preceded the American one by several years and provided an interesting example, as the Americans were deliberating what to do about the absurdly short fishing season and the race for the fish that had developed in their fishery. The European Union has a common fisheries policy; total quotas are set for the different species of fish residing in EU waters and then divided between the different members of the European Union, but the member states can choose to manage their national quota by individual quotas if they find that desirable. The Dutch have for many years had individual quotas for various kinds of flatfish, and the Danes control their fisheries by individual quotas with rules on transferability that differ between different fisheries. In Australia most fisheries have been managed by individual quotas for many years, but, again, the rules on transferability differ between fisheries. Both Chile and Peru manage some of their fisheries by individual quotas, in particular the fisheries for anchovy, which is the biggest fishery in the world, as already mentioned on several occasions. This list of quota-managed fisheries is undoubtedly incomplete and not meant to be exhaustive; there will probably be further additions as time passes.

One country, the Faeroe Islands, has abandoned management by individual transferable quotas. For two years in the 1990s the Faeroese relied on this in their fisheries for cod, haddock and saithe, but abandoned it because of pressure from the fishermen, who strongly disliked it; ever since then the Faeroese have relied on a system of limiting fishing days. It probably did not help that the quota management system was insisted on as a condition for a loan given to the near-bankrupt government of the islands by the Danish government, under whose tutelage the Faeroese have long been. However that may be, the Faeroese management by fishing days has been a failure. The basic reason is that the limit on fishing days has been set too high; in every single year since the fishing days system was put in place, the number of fishing days used has been less than the total allowed. This essentially amounts to uncontrolled fishing, and the demersal fish stocks around the islands have remained overexploited for years. Even so, the transferability of fishing licences has led to some gains in efficiency; from 1998 to 2016 the number of boats in a certain boat group in the demersal fishery declined from 161 to 77, reflecting consolidation of fishing licences on fewer boats.[9] This appears not to have reduced the pressure on the fish stocks, however, presumably because the new boats acquired on the basis of the consolidated licences are more technically advanced than the ones they replaced. This well illustrates one major difference between effort control and quota control; under effort control it can be very difficult to deal with technological progress and prevent it from translating into an undesired increase in the pressure on the fish stocks, whereas with quota control that pressure is controlled by the quota and a more efficient boat just means that the fish is captured more cheaply.

Interestingly, the Faeroese apply individual quotas in their fisheries for mackerel and herring and in their Barents Sea fisheries for cod. The amount that can be caught in these fisheries is determined by negotiations with other countries with which these stocks are shared. The Faeroese have managed to avoid the overcapacity problem in these fisheries, and they are highly profitable – so much so, in fact, that in recent years individual fish quotas have been auctioned off at high prices to individual companies.

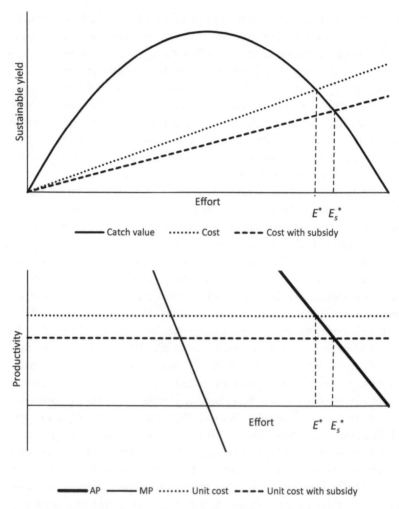

Figure 8.4 The effect of a subsidy on equilibrium effort under open access

Subsidies

The Faeroese experience also provides an interesting example of the counter-productive effects of fisheries subsidies. In the 1970s and 1980s the Faeroese government provided subsidies both to build new boats and to scrap old ones. As overcapacity developed in the fleet and fish catches declined, subsidies were provided for keeping the boats going. In the end, this nearly bankrupted the Faeroese government, as already mentioned. Fisheries subsidies are provided in many countries to support the fishing industry and to alleviate the poverty of fishermen. They may be given with the best of intentions, but in the end they are totally unproductive and likely to make a bad problem still worse. This is particularly true under the arrangement of open access that was discussed in Chapter 4. We can go back to Figure 8.2, which is reproduced with a slight modification as Figure 8.4, to illustrate the effect of subsidies. The subsidy will reduce the unit cost of fishing, as shown in the figure, but if access to the fishery is still uncontrolled this will lead to an expansion of fishing effort from the old open-access equilibrium, E^*, to a new one with the subsidy, E_s^*, and nothing will be gained in the long term. If we think of the subsidy being introduced during a temporary crisis in which the unit cost without the subsidy is higher than the average product (AP) and the subsidy allows the industry to break even, existing effort will be maintained and expanded further as normal times return. The fish stock will be further depleted and poverty in the fishery, presumably the reason for the subsidy, will be perpetuated. Price subsidies, which artificially raise the price of fish, have exactly the same kind of effect: the sustainable yield curve (in monetary terms) is displaced upwards, which for a given unit cost of effort leads to an expansion of effort. Such subsidies have been provided in many countries. In Norway this was done to a varying degree in all years from the 1950s to the 1990s. There are substantial sums of money involved; Sumaila et al. (2019) estimate "capacity enhancing subsidies" (the ones with the effect just analysed) at US$22.2 billion in 2018. All to little avail, and with negative effects on fish stocks.

Notes

1. The problems in the halibut fishery in Alaska prior to individual quotas are described in National Research Council (1999: 70–77).
2. On the Icelandic quota management system, see Arnason (1995).
3. This resulted in a report entitled *Sharing the Fish* (National Research Council 1999). The process of forming the fishery cooperatives is described at some length in Hannesson (2004).
4. Several investigations have recognized that the resource rent in quota-managed fisheries will be "hidden" in the accounts of the fishing companies in the form of financial costs for purchases of fish quotas (Flaaten, Heen & Salvanes 1995; Flaaten, Heen & Matthíasson 2017).
5. The main inspirer of this movement was Henry George with his famous book *Progress and Poverty*, first published in 1879 and reprinted several times after that (George 1997 [1879]).
6. Argentina, Australia, Brazil, Chile, France, Ecuador, New Zealand, Norway, Peru, South Africa, Spain, the United Kingdom and Uruguay.
7. On the early days of the management system in New Zealand, see Clark, Major & Mollett (1989).
8. NOAA stands for the US National Oceanic and Atmospheric Administration.
9. See Jacobsen (2019: 212), who also provides an interesting background on the Faeroese management system. See also Danielsen & Agnarsson (2018).

9
CONCLUSION

Academic fora are full of discussions about fishing as a lifestyle, tradition and culture – something to be cherished and preserved. What is left unstated, or perhaps even forgotten, is that people fish to make a living, not by eating all the fish they catch but by selling most of it to others who want it but are not in a position to catch it themselves. Any such transaction needs two parties: a willing seller and a willing buyer. In today's rich and specialized societies, the potential buyers of fish can satisfy their needs by buying fish of many different kinds and from many different sources, and perhaps not buying any fish at all but, rather, some other foodstuff they like better. Sellers of fish had better make sure they have a competitive product in terms of quality and price. If they do not, they will be unable to sell their product, and, if their culture and lifestyle are a hindrance, that will have to change.

We are all familiar with how technological progress has changed the way of life, the things we use and even our food beyond recognition. This has happened in fisheries no less than in other industries or occupations. A little over 100 years ago the most prominent British biologist at the time, Thomas Huxley, could maintain that fishing had no effect on the viability of fish populations (see Smith 1994). He was very soon to be proved wrong. Yet Huxley's thesis was entirely to the point for earlier times, before the English invented trawl fisheries and got imitated by others. Our present ability to overfish stocks so that they nearly vanish is attributable to technological progress. We touched upon this in Chapter 5, when we told the story about the Norwegian spring-spawning herring. Rapid technological progress made it possible to almost wipe out the entire fish population over just a few years.

The solution is not to reverse technological progress; that has never been a winning strategy anywhere. Rather, fish stocks must be carefully monitored and fishing activity limited to what the stocks can support. This typically means that investment in fishing boats must be limited so that the number of boats corresponds to what is needed to catch the quantity that it is allowable to take from the stocks they fish. This is what individual transferable quotas achieve, as discussed in Chapter 8. As we have seen, the allowable fish quota from any given stock can be quite variable over time, more so for some stocks than others. Fish quotas are usually determined as shares of a total allowable catch that goes up and down depending on the status of the underlying fish stock. The decision how much fishing capacity to invest in to capture large but infrequent quotas is best left to the fishing firms holding the quotas; they are the ones that have to bear the risk and thus to make the best judgement of the gains and losses involved.

Ongoing technological development typically means that fewer boats and fishermen are needed and that fish will be landed in fewer places than used to be the case. Small and isolated landing places are bound to lose out in the competition for fish landings. The fact that modern families demand a varied labour market offering opportunities to both spouses and a varied supply of services, public and private, further adds to the predicament of such places. Nevertheless, politicians often interfere with this process and try to rescue places that are losing out in the competition for the location of fishing industries and as bases for fishing boats. They may even try to breathe life into dying localities or technologies by preventing fish quotas from being sold from one location to another or from one type of boat to another. It is an uphill struggle and doomed to fail sooner or later, but those who lose from technological progress can be numerous – and they vote, providing incentives for politicians to try to stop technological progress. There is something to be said for compensating those who lose from technological progress, but putting obstacles in its way is not the way to go. Not only does it impoverish the fishing industry, it makes the whole society around it poorer as well.

Market-driven and science-based management

World fisheries are not in crisis. The stagnation in captures seems, rather, a sign that we have come to the end of the road in getting food from the sea and have drawn the adequate conclusions. More and more fish stocks are not becoming overexploited on an ever larger scale. Fisheries management has made considerable progress; some stocks have been rebuilt, others are recovering and many have been well managed for a long time. The destructive regime of open access has in many cases been replaced by regimes of limited access tailored to what the stocks can support, often by way of individual fish quotas. This has undoubtedly been facilitated by the 200-mile exclusive economic zone, which has limited the number of countries with a legitimate claim to a fish stock, sometimes to just one. It is regrettable that the community of nations has not continued along that road, eliminating loopholes where stocks are still accessible on the high seas, going instead for a decidedly second best alternative by the way of regional fisheries management organizations.

Economically, the picture may be less bright. Some countries manage their fish stocks reasonably well, but are less concerned about the economic efficiency of their fishing industry. They do not overexploit their fish stocks in a biological sense, but waste their manpower and capital on too many fishing boats or inefficient fishing boats. They may also hinder structural changes in the industry, such as vertically integrated companies, that would make the industry better equipped to compete in choosy food markets. Catching fish and landing it on the wharf is hard work, but the way from the wharf to the dinner table is long and arduous in its own way. One could say, however, that having inefficient fishing industries is a second-order problem; it harms the countries that engage in policies leading to such situations and ensures they get fewer benefits from their fish resources than they could get, but it is more important that fish stocks are well maintained and productive and contribute as much as possible to feeding mankind.

The basic weakness of fisheries policy is that it is a "policy", something decided by politicians or public administrators to whom they may delegate the task. Since policy is formulated in political circles, it falls victim to all the pressures that can be brought to bear on those who formulate policy. In this process, narrow and backward-looking self-interest may get priority over forward-looking general interest, which may not even have got much of a constituency at the time when the interest conflict is played out.

The success of the modern market economy owes much to a judicious division of labour between governments and private enterprise. Some things must be regulated by governments: the frequencies used by cellphone companies; which side of the road we should drive on; rules of commercial and non-commercial conduct must be set and enforced; dangerous products and poisonous foodstuffs must be forbidden – a complete list would be long. Then there is a large grey zone where government regulations are perhaps not necessary but do more good than harm, though some may do more harm than good. Finally, there is a large zone where companies are best left alone with their customers: deciding what to produce and how, which their customers can accept or reject. Politicians have mostly learned to stay out of that sphere, leaving companies alone to innovate and customers to accept or reject. No less importantly, there are public institutions that many governments have accepted are best left to be run by dedicated professionals with a clear mandate but independent of governments. Central banks and their setting of interest rates and other parameters of the money market are perhaps the most obvious examples.

Fisheries management should be run as an independent public institution like a central bank. It is the responsibility of governments to ensure that fish stocks are preserved at reasonable levels, not to mention their role in agreeing fish quotas and other management measures with other countries with which they share fish stocks. Stock assessment and setting targets for fish quotas should be run by professional scientists, as, indeed, is largely the case in most advanced economies. Once fish quotas and other management measures have been agreed on the basis of sound scientific principles, it should be left to the industry to decide how the permitted fish quotas are captured, where the fish are landed and for what type of processing. Interference by politicians in this process should be minimized or eliminated, as it mostly serves to offer an opportunity to those who lose out in the marketplace to redress their grievances through political manipulations. What this means in quota-managed fisheries is that quotas should be set on the basis of scientific stock assessment, while it is up to the industry and the markets in which it operates to decide how the quotas are used. This would ensure the highest possible product value consistent with the constraints set by nature.

Will the oceans feed a growing humanity?

After the Second World War world capture fisheries grew handsomely for two decades or so, and more rapidly than the world population. Thereafter, growth slowed down, and since the 1990s world capture fisheries have stagnated. The growth in fish production after that time has nevertheless been impressive and is the result of aquaculture. But marine fish are a small part of aquaculture production. No less importantly, marine aquaculture fish (including salmon) are increasingly being fed with products from the land. That is in a way not surprising, given that the capture fisheries have stagnated. There is little reason, therefore, to expect that food from the oceans will play a large role in covering the increasing need for food implied by the ever-increasing numbers of humanity. Food from the sea plays a large and in some places a vital role in the supply of food, but we cannot count on much increase in food from the sea, as the stagnation in capture fisheries and increased use of plant material in aquaculture feed prove.

A resumption of expansion in the world's capture fisheries seems to require a technological revolution of which there are no signs at the present time. It would probably require an interference in the ecosystems of the oceans that would change them beyond recognition, something akin to what we have done on land. We have chopped down our forests to give place to our cities and the farms where we grow our food. Our farms are vast areas of monocultures where unwanted plants are kept out. We have decimated predatory animals that threaten our livestock. In short, we have turned the ecological balance on land in our favour. Without this, the survival of all 7 billion of us would not be possible. One may indeed ask whether it will be at all possible, with the ecological balance we now have, to provide what in rich countries is called a decent standard of living for a world population of 7 billion, a number that is still growing, if at a declining rate. To achieve a change in the ecology of the world oceans similar to what has happened on land seems impossible, and it would in any case be highly controversial. Despite our fishing of nearly 100 million tonnes per year, the ecosystems of the oceans have been only moderately changed.

Nevertheless, concerns have been raised about our interference in the ecosystems of the oceans. We touched upon this in Chapter 3 when discussing use of sardines and anchovy for fishmeal production, most of which ends up in feed for farmed fish. Some fisheries scientists think that the captures of these species reduce the food supply for seabirds and marine mammals. This raises the question of the objectives of fish stock management. Should it be about maximizing the value of the fish taken out of the ocean, or should it be for the preservation of the ecosystem as such in a pristine or near-pristine form? These two objectives do not go well together. Should anchovies and sardines be used for supporting iconic animals or turned into fish feed? For sure, this would benefit quite different people. The benefits of preserving seabirds and marine mammals are not easily measured in terms of money, let alone cashed in and used for compensating those who would lose their livelihood in the fisheries affected by that kind of policy. If we had applied this policy of preservation to the ecosystems on land, there would not be 7 billion humans living on this planet.

REFERENCES

Alverson, D. *et al.* 1996. "A global assessment of fisheries bycatch and discards", Fisheries Technical Paper 339. Rome: Food and Agriculture Organization of the United Nations.

Anderson, L. 1973. "Optimum yield of a fishery given a variable price of output". *Journal of the Fisheries Research Board of Canada* 30: 509–18.

Anderson, L. (1985). *The Economics of Fisheries Management.* Baltimore, MD: Johns Hopkins University Press.

Arnason, R. 1995. *The Icelandic Fisheries: Evolution and Management of a Fishing Industry.* Oxford: Fishing News Books.

Asche, F., A. Cojocaru & M. Sikveland 2018. "Market shocks in salmon aquaculture: the impact of the Chilean disease crisis". *Journal of Agricultural and Applied Economics* 50(2): 255–69.

Asche, F. *et al.* 2010. "The salmon disease crisis in Chile". *Marine Resource Economics* 24: 405–11.

Barclay, K. & I. Cartwright 2007. "Governance of tuna industries: the key to economic viability and sustainability in the Western and Central Pacific Ocean". *Marine Policy* 31(3): 348–58.

Baumgartner, T., A. Soutar & V. Ferreira-Bartrina 1992. "Reconstruction of the history of Pacific sardine and northern anchovy populations over the past two millennia from sediments of the Santa Barbara Basin, California". *California Cooperative Oceanic Fisheries, Investigations Reports* 33: 24–40.

Beverton, R. & S. Holt 1957. *On the Dynamics of Exploited Fish Populations.* London: Chapman & Hall.

Bjarnason, T. & T. Thorlindsson 1993. "In defense of a 'folk model': the 'skipper effect' in the Icelandic cod fishery". *American Anthropologist* 95(2): 371–94.

Byrne, C., S. Agnarsson & B. Davidsdóttir 2019. "Profit and rent in the Icelandic harvesting sector". *Fisheries Research* 220: 105349.

Chesnokova, T. & S. McWhinnie 2019. "International fisheries access agreements and trade". *Environmental and Resource Economics* 74(3): 1207–38.

Clark, C. 1976. *Mathematical Bioeconomics.* New York: Wiley.

Clark, I., P. Major & N. Mollett 1989. "The development and implementation of New Zealand's ITQ management system". In *Rights Based Fishing*, P. Neher, R. Arnason & N. Mollett (eds), 117–52. Dordrecht: Kluwer.

189

Costello, C. *et al.* 2016. "Global fishery prospects under contrasting management regimes". *Proceedings of the National Academy of Sciences* 113(18): 5125–9.

Danielsen, R. & S. Agnarsson 2018. "Fisheries policy in the Faroe Islands: managing for failure?". *Marine Policy* 94: 204–14.

Drinkwater, K. 2002. "A review of climate variability in the decline of northern cod". *American Fisheries Society Symposium* 32: 113–30.

Einarsson, Á. 2016. *Íslenskur sjávarútvegur í alþjóðlegu samhengi* [in Icelandic]. Bifröst: University of Bifröst.

Einarsson, Á. & Á. Óladóttir 2020. *Fisheries and Aquaculture: The Food Security of the Future*. Amsterdam: Elsevier.

Ellingsen, H. & S. Aanondsen 2006. "Environmental impacts of wild caught cod and farmed salmon: a comparison with chicken". *International Journal of Life Cycle Assessment* 11(1): 60–5.

FAO 2005. "Responsible fish trade and food security", Fisheries Technical Paper 456. Rome: Food and Agriculture Organization of the United Nations.

FAO 2011. "Review of the state of world marine fishery resources", Fisheries and Aquaculture Technical Paper 569. Rome: Food and Agriculture Organization of the United Nations.

FAO 2018. *The State of World Fisheries and Aquaculture 2018: Meeting the Sustainable Development Goals*. Rome: Food and Agriculture Organization of the United Nations.

FAO 2019. *Fishery and Aquaculture Statistics 2017*. Rome: Food and Agriculture Organization of the United Nations.

FAO 2020. *The State of World Fisheries and Aquaculture 2020: Sustainability in Action*. Rome: Food and Agriculture Organization of the United Nations.

Fisheries and Oceans Canada 2019. "Stock assessment of northern (NAFO divisions 2J3KL) cod 2019", Science Advisory Report 2019/050. Ottawa: Canadian Science Advisory Secretariat.

Flaaten, O., K. Heen & T. Matthíasson 2017. "Profit and resource rent in fisheries". *Marine Resource Economics* 32(3): 311–28.

Flaaten, O., K. Heen & K. Salvanes 1995. "The invisible resource rent in limited entry and quota managed fisheries: the case of Norwegian purse seine fisheries". *Marine Resource Economics* 10(4): 341–56.

Frischmann, B., A. Marciano & G. Ramello 2019. "Tragedy of the commons after 50 years". *Journal of Economic Perspectives* 33(4): 211–28.

Garcia, S. *et al.* 2018. "Rebuilding of marine fisheries part 1: global review", Fisheries and Aquaculture Technical Paper 630/1. Rome: Food and Agriculture Organization of the United Nations.

George, H. 1997 [1879]. *Progress and Poverty*. New York: Robert Schalkenbach Foundation.

Gibbons, R. 1992. *A Primer in Game Theory*. Hemel Hempstead: Harvester Wheatsheaf.

Golubtsov, P. & R. McKelvey 2007. "The incomplete information split-stream fish war: examining the implications of competing risks". *Natural Resource Modeling* 20(2): 263–300.

Gonner, E. 1966 [1912]. *Common Land and Inclosure*, 2nd edn. Abingdon: Frank Cass.

Gordon, D. & R. Hannesson 2015. "The Norwegian winter herring fishery: a story of technological progress and stock collapse". *Land Economics* 91: 362–85.

Gordon, D., K. Salvanes & F. Atkins 1994. "A fish is a fish is a fish? Testing for market linkages on the Paris fish market". *Marine Resource Economics* 8, 331–43.

Hannesson, R. 1978. *Economics of Fisheries: An Introduction*. Bergen: Universitetsforlaget.

Hannesson, R. 2002. "The economics of fisheries". In *Handbook of Fish Biology and Fisheries*, vol. 2, *Fisheries*, P. Hart & J. Reynolds (eds), 249–69. Oxford: Blackwell.

Hannesson, R. 2004. *The Privatization of the Oceans.* Cambridge, MA: MIT Press.

Hannesson, R. 2007. "Incentive compatibility of fish-sharing agreements". In *Advances in Fisheries Economics: Festschrift in Honour of Professor Gordon R. Munro,* T. Bjørndal (ed.), 196–206. Oxford: Blackwell.

Hannesson, R. 2020. "The Nash–Cournot approach to shared fish stocks: an empirical investigation". *Marine Policy* 118: 103978.

Hardin, G. 1968. "The tragedy of the commons". *Science* 162: 1243–8.

Havice, E. 2010. "The structure of tuna access agreements in the Western and Central Pacific ocean: lessons for vessel day scheme planning". *Marine Policy* 34(5): 979–87.

Hilborn, R. *et al.* 2017. "When does fishing forage species affect their predators?". *Fisheries Research* 191: 211–21.

Hill, K., P. Crone & J. Zwolinski 2019. "Assessment of the Pacific sardine resource in 2019 for US management in 2019–20", Technical Memorandum NMFS-SWFSC 615. La Jolla, CA: National Oceanic and Atmospheric Administration Southwest Fisheries Science Center.

Hutchings, J. & R. Meyers 1994. "What can be learned from the collapse of a renewable resource? Atlantic cod, *Gadus morhua,* of Newfoundland and Labrador". *Canadian Journal of Fisheries and Aquatic Sciences* 51: 2126–46.

ICES 2019a. "Arctic fisheries working group", Scientific Report 1:30. Copenhagen: International Council for the Exploration of the Sea.

ICES 2019b. "Working group on widely distributed stocks (WGWIDE)", Scientific Report 1:36. Copenhagen: International Council for the Exploration of the Sea.

Jacobsen, J. 2019. "Path dependence in Faroese fisheries (mis)management". *Marine Policy* 108: 103615.

Jacobson, L. & A. MacCall 1995. "Stock-recruitment models for Pacific sardine (*Sardinops sagax*)". *Canadian Journal of Fisheries and Aquatic Sciences* 52: 566–77.

Jang, H., S. Yamazaki & E. Hoshino 2019. "Profit and equity trade-offs in the management of small pelagic fisheries: the case of the Japanese sardine fishery", Discussion Paper 2019-03. Hobart: University of Tasmania.

Kazcynski, V. & D. Fluharty 2002. "European policies in West Africa: who benefits from fisheries agreements?". *Marine Policy* 26(2): 75–93.

Lenfest Ocean Program 2012. *Little Fish, Big Impact: Managing a Crucial Link in Ocean Food Webs.* Washington, DC: Lenfest Ocean Program.

Løbach, T. *et al.* 2020. "Regional fisheries management organizations and advisory bodies: activities and developments, 2000–2017", Fisheries and Aquaculture Technical Paper 651. Rome: Food and Agriculture Organization of the United Nations.

Mallory, T. 2013. "China's distant water fishing industry: evolving policies and implications". *Marine Policy* 38: 99–108.

Mowi 2019. *Salmon Farming Industry Handbook.* Bergen: Mowi. Available at https://corpsite.azureedge.net/corpsite/wp-content/uploads/2019/06/Salmon-Industry-Handbook-2019.pdf.

National Research Council 1999. *Sharing the Fish: Toward a National Policy on Individual Fishing Quotas.* Washington, DC: National Academy Press.

Naylor, R. *et al.* 2006. "Feeding aquaculture in an era of finite resources". *Proceedings of the National Academy of Sciences of the United States of America* 106(36): 15103–10.

Óskarsson, G. 2018. "The existence and population connectivity of Icelandic spring-spawning herring over a 50-year collapse period". *ICES Journal of Marine Science* 75(6): 2025–32.

Österblom, H. *et al.* 2015. "Transnational corporations as 'keystone actors' in marine ecosystems". *PLOS ONE* 10(5): e0127533.

Pérez Roda, M. *et al.* 2019. "A third assessment of global marine fisheries discards", Fisheries and Aquaculture Technical Paper 633. Rome: Food and Agriculture Organization of the United Nations.

Pintassilgo, P. *et al.* 2010. "Stability and success of regional fisheries management organizations". *Environmental and Resource Economics* 46(3): 377–402.

Pitcher, T. & P. Hart 1982. *Fisheries Ecology*. London: Croom Helm.

Ricker, W. 1958. *Handbook of Computations for Biological Statistics of Fish Populations*. Ottawa: Fisheries Research Board of Canada.

Ricker, W. 1975. *Computation and Interpretation of Biological Statistics of Fish Populations*. Ottawa: Department of Environment, Fisheries and Marine Service.

Samró, Ó. 2016. *Fiskiskapur: Fjølbreyttar ásetningar [Fisheries: Multiple Objectives]*. Thorshavn: Óli Samró.

Schaefer, M. (1954). "Some aspects of the dynamics of populations important to the management of the commercial marine fisheries". *Inter-American Tropical Tuna Commission Bulletin* 1, 27–56.

Smith, T. 1994. *Scaling Fisheries: The Science of Measuring the Effects of Fishing, 1855–1955*. Cambridge: Cambridge University Press.

Sumaila, R. *et al.* 2019. "Updated estimates and analysis of global fisheries subsidies". *Marine Policy* 109: 103695.

Tahvonen, O. 2009. "Economics of harvesting age-structured fish populations". *Journal of Environmental Economics and Management* 58(3): 281–99.

Tingley, G. & M. Dunn 2018. "Global review of orange roughy (*Hoplostethus atlanticus*), their fisheries, biology and management", Fisheries and Aquaculture Technical Paper 622. Rome: Food and Agriculture Organization of the United Nations.

Toresen, R. & O. Østvedt 2000. "Variation in abundance of Norwegian spring-spawning herring (*Clupea harengus, Clupeidae*) throughout the 20th century and the influence of climatic fluctuations". *Fish and Fisheries* 1(3): 231–56.

Toresen, R. *et al.* 2019. "Sudden change in long-term ocean climate fluctuations corresponds with ecosystem alterations and reduced recruitment in Norwegian spring-spawning herring (*Clupea harengus, Clupeidae*)". *Fish and Fisheries* 20(4): 686–96.

Ulltang, Ø. 1980. "Factors affecting the reaction of pelagic fish stocks to exploitation and requiring a new approach to assessment and management". *Conseil International pour l'Exploration de la Mer, Rapport et Procès-Verbaux des Réunions* 177: 489–504.

Weitzman, M. 2002. "Landing fees vs harvest quotas for uncertain fish stocks". *Journal of Environmental Economics and Management* 43(2): 325–38.

WorldFish Center 2011. "Aquaculture, fisheries, poverty and food security", Working Paper 2011–65. Penang: WorldFish Center.

Yaragina, N., B. Bogstad & Y. Kovalyev 2009. "Variability in cannibalism in northeast Arctic cod (*Gadus morhua*) during the period 1947–2006". *Marine Biology Research* 5(1): 75–85.

LIST OF FIGURES AND TABLES

Figures

Tables

INDEX